Marianne Straub

MARY SCHOESER

The Design Council

With thanks (16 years late)
to a dedicated teacher
Floyd W. Jones

Marianne Straub

First edition published in the United Kingdom
1984 by The Design Council, 28 Haymarket
London SW1Y 4SU

Phototypesetting by Trutapes
Margate, Kent

Printed and bound in the United Kingdom by
The Whitefriars Press Ltd

British Library CIP Data

Schoeser, Mary
  Marianne Straub
  1. Textile design—Great Britain
  I. Title
  677'022'0941   NK8843

ISBN 0-85072-153-9

Contents

Preface

A full time designer in a company is a member of a team which is responsible for keeping a factory in work. To find a balance between, on the one hand, the dictates of fashion, the manufacturing facilities available and the firm's sales policy and, on the other hand, the individual's design standards is by no means an easy task. My principle was always to attempt to achieve the best result within my ability, whilst following the general demand as far as necessary, welcoming the occasional contract orders which allowed greater design freedom and which tended to be less tightly budgeted. I took up the opportunity to become involved in teaching with considerable doubt at my ability to pass on the knowledge I had acquired in the course of the years spent in the textile industry. But I soon discovered it to be a stimulating, very rewarding task. In the context of my educational activities I have been able to extend my interests, and have now the time to explore the seemingly unlimited field of woven and allied constructed textiles. I have found the combination of designing for industry and teaching ideal, the one imposing a healthy discipline, the other opening up a wide horizon. It has been a happy life in a profession which is all absorbing because its scope is so wide. My love for and interest in all forms of textiles has never waned, and I hope that I have been able to pass it on to some students and young colleagues.

Woven cloth, indeed any form of textiles (excepting the rare few of great value from the outset) have never been collector's items. By the time they have served their years in the use for which they were made, they tend to be pale and frail shadows of their original colour and quality. There may be reference samples and cuttings, carefully preserved in the record books. But how can these convey the rhythm of a design, the boldness of the colouring and the fall and handle of the cloth? To make matters worse, a cloth relates to its use; it only becomes 'alive' when it is seen in the context of its purpose. Photographs of textiles may provide valuable contextual information but are often difficult to locate or identify. I know that the author, Mary Schoeser, agrees with these sentiments, for the book has been planned to coincide with an exhibition of the textiles which I have created during the last 50 years, the majority of them designed for industrial production and some handwoven individually. Whilst it has been a relatively easy task to piece together my life story, the author has been faced with the unenviable and far harder task of locating background information and of designing and assembling the exhibition. We also agree that a book with illustrations which can give only little tactile impression of textiles or an exhibition of textiles divorced from their function have to be looked at with imagination and sympathy to bring them alive. The combination greatly increases the validity of each, and I would like to thank Warner & Sons Ltd for generously organising the exhibition (and for maintaining an archive of their production — wisely preserving as many colourways, designs and records as possible).

I am aware that, simply by chance, I am the first textile designer to be chosen for this series of monographs on the work of industrial designers. It is not necessarily a measure of my standing among my professional colleagues. Nevertheless, this does not diminish my appreciation of having been chosen by The Design Council, and to all concerned I extend my thanks. Finally, I wish to acknowledge my debt of gratitude to my teacher, Heinz Otto Hürlimann, and to the many friends who have supported and encouraged me in my work.

Marianne Straub
Cambridge, November 1983

Marianne Straub

Introduction

As personalities, first-rate sculptors and weavers have always held a very high place in my esteem. They have mastered the challenge of an enormous range of techniques, and know their materials intimately in order to express to the full their creative ideas. As a result they seem to acquire a dedication and humility which only a lifetime's commitment, lovingly borne, can impart. It is a privilege, therefore, to be invited to introduce Mary Schoeser's account of the apprenticeship and working life of Marianne Straub, the finest designer of woven fabrics in this country at the present. New generations of highly skilled specialist craftsmen have grown up during her life; what sets Marianne apart is that she chose at a very early stage to become a designer for industry.

I was 23 when I first interviewed her shortly after she had become Managing Director of Helios Fabrics in 1948. She must have been a very busy woman, but she spared no time or pains in her efforts to explain to me the weave designer's task and her own approach to it. We sat for hours on the floor of her studio in Bolton with weave diagrams, yarns and point paper around us. Perhaps I was young enough to regard such kindness almost as my due; only later did I realise the extent to which Marianne's enthusiasm to impart her knowledge was the highest possible compliment she could have paid me. I can still recall her lively bird-like intensity and the quickness of her smile when she realised that I had grasped a point: there was no self-consciousness, no boastfulness, simply the genuine enthusiast's eagerness to communicate her unique comprehension of structure and technique to a receptive mind.

Newly appointed to take editorial responsibility for the glossy overseas edition of *Fashions and Fabrics,* I found myself increasingly involved in the creative aspects of design, and of textiles in particular. Having interviewed Marianne Straub in Bolton, Margaret Leischner in London and Theo Moorman in Leeds, as well as having talked to Alec Hunter at Warners and to Alastair Morton, I was struck that each had emphasised the prime importance of yarn as a source of inspiration, as well as the medium of a weaver. This unanimity took me by surprise. Indeed, my original title for the article which I developed from these talks ('Designing from the Yarn Up') was intended to make this fundamental clear to the non-specialist also. In her lecture at the Dartington Hall Conference in 1952 Marianne herself stressed yarn as the crucial element:

'I always feel rather unhappy about the word "design" because it sounds so super-imposed . . . By design I mean the pattern that is made by the interlacing of the threads. And can there be anything lovelier than a material woven, one thread up and one thread down with the right yarns? There is nothing to compete with the character of the thread, and the shadows produced through the simple interlacing of the yarn gives such depth and vibration to the cloth.'

While I was at the Cotton Board Design Centre from 1948 to 1964, Marianne's work was featured in most of the exhibitions of the work of the Textile Group of the Society of Industrial Artists and in the exhibition of textiles and other products by their members which I also staged in Manchester. I came to know well her work for Helios and Warners during these years and Marianne's fabrics were always truly of their time. She was adept in the use of a wide variety of novelty yarns. Her understanding of the medium was complete. She could visualise a fabric with such accuracy that she only needed to write the weave instructions or draw up a point paper design for her colleagues. Mary Schoeser indicates how this mastery was acquired through intensive application and study, and how it developed further as the years progressed. To each new experience Marianne brought an uncommon blend of skills which she was able to broaden further by the special nature of her previous experiences.

It would be presumptuous of me to attempt to analyse her design development over a lifetime, but her range of skills — from the masterly use of innumerable fancy yarns for Helios in the 1940s to the sophisticated simplicity of her designs at Warners for Tamesa in the 1960s alone — illustrates her ability to anticipate and respond to the demands made on an industrial designer of woven textiles serving differing markets and changing tastes. Marianne's response to change and her readiness to relish the best of others' work has become more and more marked with the years. To appreciate how well attuned she was, how brilliant at absorbing the needs of both manufacturers and clients and producing cloth of the right character at the right time, one must appreciate the rapid and demanding changes which the textile industry underwent between 1930 and 1970. This appreciation the author provides, beginning with the background to Marianne's early work with the Welsh Mills. It was arduous and often frustrating, but this experience introduced her to the requirements of furniture manufacturers and earned their respect which she retained throughout her working life. The author mentions the unique 'club' formed by these firms, a handful of retailers, and the Warners, the Mortons and the Barlows from the 1930s onwards. Marianne rapidly became a valued member of this world and a valued friend of the designers who moved through it.

In charting the previously little documented relationships of the 'club', Mary Schoeser is broadening the scope of our understanding of British textile history. She is also making clear why much of Marianne's early work appeared anonymously. When I furnished my first flat in Manchester in the early 1950s, I did so almost entirely with furniture from the range of Howard Keith and Ernest Race, for whom Marianne designed so many exclusive uncredited fabrics. Something similar happened in Birmingham in 1965 when I furnished my first modern flat, which had huge windows crying out for a sympathetic reflection of the surrounding trees. I did so using Tamesa fabrics exclusively. Hans Tisdall's sage-on-white leaf-stripe print, 'Alexandria', made two curtains which swept across the 18 foot main window, where a number of adjustable woven curtains in a creamy 'Echo Stripe' could be used to shield the room from bright sunlight or to give a warm natural glow in less cheerful weather. 'Echo Check', woven in white on sage, was my choice for the bedroom curtains and 'Echo Check', in sage on cream, for the dining room. I realise now that these must have been from Isabel Tisdall's first collection, and I am not even sure if at that stage I knew who had designed the weaves, let alone where they had been woven. It says much for the lasting qualities of the weaves that, while my present canal-side cottage proved too small to accommodate their scale, some continue in active use by a colleague. What is undeniable is how well co-ordinated the range was, how superbly the colours of the prints and weaves were related, and how justified were the architects of the time in being so warm in their reception.

We learn early how Marianne's interest in colour and texture began. The limitation of technical education of women in Switzerland and her study with Heinz Otto Hürlimann gave her initially both a strong Bauhaus ethic and an urge to seek greater technical knowledge in England. In addition, possibly influenced by childhood misfortunes, she was driven by an intense desire to learn which was, perhaps, further strengthened by her frequently finding herself a woman in a man's world — a situation of which Marianne was often able to take full advantage. An early memory of her discussing 'everything' with three small boys while in hospital is, to me, both touching and typical. Her urge to learn was equalled by her willingness to share her knowledge, as she did with me and many others later, as a teacher. Her teaching first began at Gospels, and it is hard to say who gained most from Marianne's long association with Ethel Mairet. Marianne, with her greater technical resource, enlarged the Gospels' range of fabrics tremendously, but the fundamental craft base of the Gospels' work allowed her to extend a well developed colour sense through dyeing with natural dyes and to increase her understanding of yarns by hand spinning. In the year of Ethel Mairet's death, 1952, Marianne was to acknowledge that her own '. . . love is in the craft' and that without her own spinning wheel and her own handloom she '. . . could never go on weaving. It would just become duller and duller.' Marianne was by then well established as an industrial designer and '. . . had been able from that position to appreciate what the craftsman is trying to do and is struggling for.'

Her appreciation of excellence and the warmth she feels for the truly creative spirit is always very much apparent. When, in the mid-1960s, as Head of Fashion and Textiles at Birmingham, we endeavoured to extend our DipAD course in Woven Textiles (which Marianne assessed) to embrace other forms of construction — particularly knitting — I remember her expressing some reserve, some feeling that this was perhaps too easy an option. In the tributes to her as a teacher since then, it is delightful to note how many come from designers who have specialised with outstanding success in this area. The same appreciation was apparent when I first visited her at Great Bardfield, in her immense concern that I should miss none of the work of her neighbours. It is illustrated best by her own words, spoken in relation to her work at Warners:

'I am fortunate in having in the works an old Spitalfields weaver who, because he was lonely and bored at home — he is over 70 — has come back to work as my assistant. Do you know, the knowledge that man has has given me a tremendous lot to think about. Whatever problem I come up against I go to my Mr Spinks. . . . on the other hand, he came to me the other day and said: . . . "I have learned an awful lot from you because you do things so differently." And there it is, you see. We all have to give . . . and we must help each other, and we must keep that tradition alive because it is a most valuable one.'

Today, when Marianne and I meet at a student exhibition, at the Royal Society of Arts or the Crafts Council, she continues to give everything she sees careful appraisal. She misses nothing of importance which is going on — not only in the area of industrial design but in the increasingly significant world of education and textile crafts, which she has done so much to foster in recent years. Her abilities have been recognised in many ways, among them (and most appropriately) the Royal Society's award of the title 'Royal Designer for Industry' in 1972. Marianne wears her distinguished eminence lightly. Her vigour seems undiminished. That she still has the scrubbed, tanned look of the eager child, which Mary Schoeser's early illustrations convey, seems somehow inevitable rather than extraordinary.

Donald Tomlinson
November 1983

Marianne Straub

Early life

Marianne Straub was born on 23 September 1909 in Amriswil, a Swiss village not far from Lake Constance (Fig 1.1). Her father was a textile yarn merchant and her mother, in the Swiss tradition, was well versed in tatting, embroidery, sewing and knitting. A visitor to the Straubs some years later found '. . . a large very spacious house [with] beautifully polished floors everywhere — big garden — lovely kitchen, copper sinks. They have one maid, German, and do a great deal of housework, cooking etc.' There was also a farm '. . . (which Herr Straub ran as a hobby) with 16 cows, many bells, two horses for getting in the hay' and, of course, for riding.[1]

Although the second oldest among four girls, her early influences were not to be from her family, but from the environment of the hospital where she was treated for tuberculosis from the age of 3½ to 8 (Fig 1.2). Much of this time she was immobilised by traction and dependent upon her hands and imagination for amusement. Her memories of this small, secure world are happy ones:

'I shared the room with three lovely boys and we discussed *everything*. We all had the same wonderful imaginative power — we could build our imaginary world and I'm sure that was a great asset.'[2]

Initially, she could do little but play with Plasticine and a few crayons so that, by the time she left hospital and went to school, colour and texture had become great interests. These were gradually expanded to include a delight in yarns

Fig 1.1 The Straub family home in Amriswil as it appeared c1930.

1 Ethel Mairet Travel Journal 'Switzerland', 25 June–2 July 1938 pp3–4, Craft Study Centre, Bath.
2 Taped interview (no 1) with Marianne Straub, 25 March 1983. All information from taped interviews was subsequently edited by Marianne Straub. Many quotes were prompted by information from taped interviews to which Marianne responded in writing. These are denoted in further footnotes by 'Marianne Straub' and all originated between 15 August and 14 November 1983.

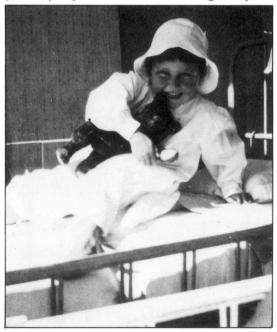

Fig 1.2 Marianne Straub in hospital in 1913, aged 4.

and their manipulation when, a few years later during a short hospital visit, she was given a bead loom. Later still, at the age of 12 or 13, she had a further six months of enforced inactivity and requested a narrow strip loom such as she had seen at her aunt's. Although the loom was capable only of plain cloths, to this she added adventurous colour combinations and areas of brocading. Her mother taught her to knit, and she was soon exploring the possibilities of making a variety of patterns and textures. Her memory for both was acute and she was able to recall any group of knitting stitches simply by the mention of them. Together she and her mother made jumpers for her sisters, sometimes working as a team in which she completed the patterned areas and her mother the plain.

When she began her formal schooling at the age of nine, Marianne Straub found that she loved maths, but disliked reading and the formal sewing and knitting lessons, which she found 'a bit dull' (Fig 1.3). She became a very keen swimmer, going frequently by brake to Lake Constance with her parents and sisters, each of whom developed a great fondness for the chang-ing mood and colour of the water and its surroundings. Although Lake Constance is now a popular spot, where many Swiss have bought

land and beach huts, the Straub family was one of the first to regularly enjoy evening picnics and swims. The magic of the lake has remained potent, for whenever Marianne Straub visits her home in Switzerland, inevitably she and her sister Ruth return to its shores (Fig 1.4).

By the time she was 15, she had formulated the idea that she would study textiles further, but it was not until she went to boarding school in Celerina, in the Engadin, where she met a girl who shared her interest in the crafts, that she decided to go to art school. Together they formulated their plans to attend the *Kunstgewerbeschule* in Zurich, Marianne Straub to study weaving and her friend to study book binding.

She recalls the entrance exams clearly — in 1928 an arduous, two day event. The first morning's interview was undertaken by Sophie Teuber, wife of Jean Arp and a constructivist artist and fine embroideress. Sophie Teuber asked the prospective students to do a drawing from memory, the subject of which was to be something from childhood — and Marianne Straub drew a single line of beds! She had for a time during secondary school gone for drawing lessons to a distant relation who was a retired art master, but did not regard drawing as her

Fig 1.3 Marianne Straub (top right) with her classmates in 1920.

Fig 1.4 Lake Constance, on the Swiss–German border.

strongest skill. However, she and Sophie Teuber got on well at the subsequent personal interview, establishing a rapport which would not be developed because the latter had at that point resigned her teaching appointment. Marianne Straub believed she would have been a great inspiration, and for many years afterwards cherished a silk embroidered guitar band made by Sophie Teuber, a Christmas present from her parents some years before. The entrance exam also included a morning of pottery and an afternoon writing an essay. She had been 'tipped' that the content of the essay was less important than the layout of the page, and therefore knew that the examiners were seeking a demonstration of a visual sense. To her delight, she was accepted (Fig 1.5).

The first year of the course was a general art training, including several days' drawing, hand-built pottery, clay modelling and lettering. Most stimulating were the drawing classes with Otto Meyer Amden, and she also became interested in Edward Johnston's books on lettering, which had recently been published in German.[3] Some years later, when at Gospels, Marianne Straub met Johnston and, her interest in lettering still alive, was allowed to visit his house nearby to look at his work.

The second and third years were devoted entirely to hand weaving and took place in the basement of the Silk Industry's *Seidenwebschule,* a building some distance from the main college (Fig 1.6). While the art school's weaving students

Fig 1.5 Marianne Straub while an art student in Zurich, c1927.

Fig 1.6 The Zurich silk industry's Seidenwebschule *in the basement of which was the hand-weaving department of the art college.*

3   Johnston's most widely published book was *Writing and Illuminating and Lettering,* first published in London in 1906 and in its 19th edition by 1942.

were therefore somewhat separated from their colleagues in other disciplines, they had the advantage of getting at least an occasional glimpse of what was going on upstairs on the powerlooms. The weaving equipment was adequate, consisting of countermarch looms and dobbies, together with one drawloom working on the damask principle. However the students had no opportunity to dye their yarn nor to learn to spin. All yarn was bought-in in a dyed state.

The weaving course of the art school was under the sole care and tuition of Heinz Otto Hürlimann, a young man who had studied at the Bauhaus in 1920–21. His teaching was quite unorthodox:

> 'We had no planned tuition as such. We were given what help we needed to discover what a loom set up with a certain draft and pedal tie-up could do. Hürlimann only came to our assistance when asked. A great deal of the experimentation was directed towards discovering weave textures and working on subtle colour changes by altering the proportion of warp–weft relationships. Every piece which came off the loom was hung up and critically discussed by master and pupils. After careful planning of the next piece of work it would be presented for approval to Hürlimann too, but at that stage little criticism was voiced, for we were to discover for ourselves where we had failed in our planning. It was a demanding form of teaching, most valuable for those who had their craft deeply at heart, but I fear it left a fair number of casualties on the way.'[4]

Whilst the weave students were encouraged to develop their own talent they were, in the Bauhaus tradition, made aware of contemporary developments. Their fabrics were to relate to the architecture, art and design of the day, and no thought was given to ethnic or historical influ-ences. 'Borrowing' ideas was considered a moral weakness.

From Hürlimann (Fig 1.7) Marianne Straub acquired her highly critical eye, which he encouraged in his students through the intensive critiques on all work as it came off the looms. All teaching staff at the *Kunstgewerbeschule* were employed on a part-time basis, and all were practising artists and craftsmen within their own

KRISTEN KNELL

Fig 1.7 Herr Hürlimann, photographed by a Kunstgewerbeschule *textile student on a study trip to Italy, c1960.*

4   Taped interview (no 1) with Marianne Straub, *op cit.*

studio/workshops. Hürlimann maintained himself through his own studio where he wove various types of rugs and domestic furnishings. In later years he moved to a small hand-weaving establishment in the Appenzellerland where he had the use of swivel looms. Rug weaving by this time had been abandoned, their place taken by Jacquard-woven tablecloths, curtains and upholstery cloths for an interior decorator and swivel loom woven cloths for ties, dresses and shawls. Marianne Straub was given the opportunity to spend some of the holiday periods in Hürlimann's studio. Later, after the war, while on an extended holiday in Switzerland, she was invited to return to the studio, where she was able to explore the design scope the swivel loom mechanism offered.

The characteristic of the swivel loom was that it was able to carry a number of shuttles entered at intervals across the warp so that areas of different colours could be woven as a constituent

Fig 1.8 A fine woollen swivel loom woven scarf designed by Hürlimann for the Swiss National Exhibition in 1964.

part of the cloth rather than as an additional inlaid, or brocaded motif (Fig 1.8). The resulting light weight of the cloth could be further enhanced by allowing vertical slits to occur, as in tapestry. The loom was a hand operated Jacquard, with no potential for mechanisation and thus well suited to cottage industry. Prior to the war there were still hundreds of swivel looms in the villages around Zurich, a typical workshop employing five or six men and women and 10–12 looms. The designs and materials were supplied to the weavers, who were paid by the piece.[5] Many worked to traditional designs which had also found their way into Swiss embroideries, but the loom was extremely flexible and, with it, Hürlimann explored the use of new cloth constructions and materials. In 1938 Marianne Straub and Ethel Mairet visited Hürlimann in his studio and at the art school, after which Ethel Mairet wrote, 'Herr Hürlimann would be a good teacher: he is an artist [and] knows gauze techniques well.'[6]

Whilst studying at Zurich, Marianne Straub developed a great interest in the theatre. She never missed a new production at the *Schauspielhaus,* and would pay a repeat visit if the play seemed of particular merit or the scenery of special interest. When she was in her third year at the College an opportunity arose to attend a newly created one-day-a-week class in stage design. The course was taken by Ernst Gubler, a sculptor and excellent motivator. She was doubly fortunate to be invited to attend Gubler's course, for it was originally restricted to young men only, and it became the setting for what Marianne Straub regards as '. . . a most important stage in my development.'

The breakthrough came with Marianne

5 Ethel Mairet Travel Journal, *op cit* p12.
6 *Ibid.* Hürlimann, born in 1900, taught at the *Kunstgewerbeschule* from 1927 until the year before his death in 1963.

Straub's models for a puppet theatre based on a play by Claudelle. Set within a prison cell, the characters consisted of the prisoner and an inspirational figure who visits him. Marianne Straub made the clothes and wigs for the puppets, and these, together with the model, were shortly afterwards exhibited in an international exhibition of theatre design held in Zurich. She recalls of the experience:

'The break with the specialisation in cloth constructions and the discipline of designing woven cloth had a quite unexpected effect on me. I discovered a new world of creative activities, a freedom of using light, texture and colour without the restrictions which rule the viability of the cloth. Suddenly the work began to blossom; ideas came flooding in and with it a confidence which had been sadly lacking in my work before. It affected my textile design work and without doubt my whole future career. After that I *knew* I could do it.'[7]

There was a puppet theatre attached to the art school, where a professional puppeteer and student assistants performed to the public two months in every winter. Marianne Straub participated as a speaker, and this interest made a great change in her student life. Her fellow final-year weaving students numbered only three, with an additional two or three in the second year. Thus the chance to break away from the isolation of the weaving school was welcomed.

By her third year she had decided to become an industrial weaver, wishing to '. . . design things which people who were not rich could afford'[8] because '. . . to remain a handweaver did not seem satisfactory in this age of mass production.'[9] However, she did set up a 16 shaft dobby loom in her own studio for a short time, completing a few commissions (cotton and linen bedspreads, curtains and cushion covers) (Fig 1.9) while looking

for an opportunity to extend her training. Neither of the two Swiss textile colleges would accept women on their courses at that time, so when the opportunity came to work in a small local weaving mill she gladly accepted the offer.

Thus Marianne Straub began her 'shop floor' work as a technician's assistant at a local mill, Maurer's *Weberei* in Amriswill, where for six months in 1931–32 she learned to handle the machines, which included a very complex loom with two dobbies. The mill produced domestic textiles, such as thick cleaning cloths, towels etc, and Marianne Straub acted as technician and handiman while carrying out her tasks of wind-

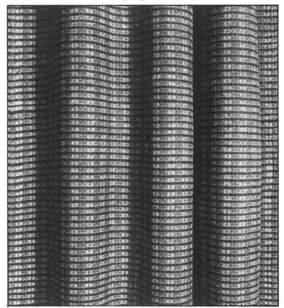

Fig 1.9 Curtain made by Marianne Straub in Switzerland, 1931.

7 Marianne Straub, *op cit.*
8 Coleman, Marigold 'A Weaver's Life', *Crafts* May/June 1978, p39.
9 Great Bardfield Summer Exhibition catalogue, 8–17 July 1955, p19.

ing, warping and weaving. She has said of her experience at the *Weberei:*

> 'I was given the most temperamental loom in the weaving shed to look after. Whenever the power got a bit low, the shuttle tended to fly out, always to the right, into a wood-fired stove which was quite pitted by the numerous impacts from the shuttle. I was terrified, and had nightmares about it, but learned a lot.'[10]

At the end of the six months she was 'paid' with twelve towels — 'worth *every* penny!' It was during this period that she heard through a family friend about the courses at Bradford Technical College, and decided to apply. It was perhaps her experiences in childhood that gave her the independence and determination to undertake study in Bradford, for she had learned during her long years in hospital that '. . . others could be just as kind as her family.'

One must remember, too, that although Hürlimann never undertook industrial production, through him Marianne Straub had been imbued with the Bauhaus ideal, summed up by its then ex-director, Walter Gropius, in 1934:

> The Bauhaus accepted the machine as the essentially modern vehicle of form, and sought to come to terms with it. Its workshops were really laboratories in which practical designs for present-day goods were conscientiously worked out as models for mass production, and were continually being improved on. This dominant aim of creating type-forms to meet every commercial, technical, and aesthetic requirement necessitated a picked body of men of all-round culture who were thoroughly experienced in the practical and mechanical, as well as the theoretical, scientific and formal aspects of design, and were

well versed in the laws on which these are based. The constructors of these models had also to be fully acquainted with factory methods of mechanical mass-production, which are radically different from those of handicraft, although the various parts of the prototypes they evolved had naturally to be made by hand. It is from the individual peculiarities of every type of machine that the new, but still individual 'genuineness' and 'beauty' of its products are derived.'[11]

To meet this ideal, Marianne Straub needed to extend her knowledge of designing handwovens and her experience of mill work to include the mechanical, theoretical and scientific understanding of powerloom weaving which Bradford could offer. She was undeterred by the fact that Bradford addressed their correspondence to 'Mr Straub' and was duly accepted. Upon leaving the mill at the end of March 1932, she spent a month in the south of France with relatives and by August was in London, improving her English and visiting museums and galleries.

Bradford Technical College

When Marianne Straub arrived in Bradford in September 1932, the staff of the college were somewhat surprised to find that she was not Mr but Miss Straub. Although two women had attended the college previously, she was the only female on the course at the time and acknowledges that this, together with her interest in the machinery, granted her preferential treatment, which she exploited to gain as much knowledge as possible.

10   Coleman, *op cit* p39.
11   Gropius, Walter, 'The formal and technical problems of modern architecture and planning', *Journal of the Royal Institute of British Architects,* 19 May 1934, vol. 31, no 13, p682.

The curriculum at the college offered depth and breadth in the study of powerloom production, for the textile department had been created for and was supported by the local textile industry, which largely produced woollen cloths. From very early in the century the college offered various modes of study, including evening classes and tailor-made short courses for specialised study not leading to the diploma. It was the second of these options that Marianne Straub pursued. Because of her previous experience she was placed with the second year students and followed an individual course, designed to encompass three years of cloth construction studies.

With Mr Oversby she studied textile maths, with Mr Wilkinson, spinning, and with Mr Kershaw, raw materials. Mr Kershaw was one of the lecturers who greatly influenced her, for he instilled in his student his interest in sheep breeds and the endless variety of wool fibres. Today she still continues to add to her collection of wool samples started at Bradford. However, it was Mr

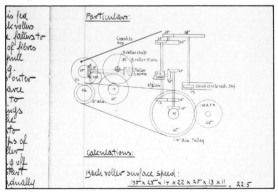

Fig 1.10 A page from 'Yarn Manufacturers, Lectures II' notebook kept by Marianne Straub while a student in Bradford. The diagram shows a Lister nip comb for separating long fibres from short fibres for making worsted yarn. The calculations indicate the speed of the rollers.

Healey, who taught weaving technology, and Mr Tindall who taught cloth construction, who had the greatest impact of her subsequent work as an industrial designer. Mr Healey quickly found how to motivate her:

'On Saturday morning the teacher of weaving technology and the technical staff played a sort of game with me, upsetting the mechanism of the loom and then asking me to find the fault — the best game of "hide and seek" I ever played.'[12]

Marianne Straub's notebooks from this course show an intense delight in the detailed workings of textile machinery, including meticulous drawings and diagrams of every machine she studied (Fig 1.10). She was aware that only by understanding the scope of the various types of looms thoroughly would she be able to gain the maximum design freedom.

Her most intensive study was with Mr Tindall, in cloth construction. Again the notebooks are detailed, and virtually all types of weaves are covered. Although she had learned doublecloth constructions in Zurich, it was at Bradford that she began to investigate this weave in greater depth. Tindall was to remark to her that he had never known anyone who took to it so naturally, and it has remained the weave that consistently appears in Marianne Straub's work. The variations possible in doublecloth are immense, and her use of this weave is so wide-ranging that the resultant cloths have in common only their structure, and seldom their appearance.[13]

It was at Bradford that Marianne Straub's highly developed powers of abstract reasoning became apparent — what she refers to as her 'television box'. As one does in calculus, she could start once she had the 'answer', only then returning to the beginning to determine the 'equation'. The solution to any design problem always included visualising the fabric in context to achieve the right scale and draping or wearing qualities. Although her Jacquard designs were drawn out, designs for the dobby were produced directly on the handloom, a habit which she continued throughout her work as a designer for industrial production.

Of her life at college, Marianne Straub recalls that it was largely taken up with work, which was:

> 'Wonderful . . . paradise! — *hard* work but worth it. I learned *so* much, they were so kind to me, probably because I was from abroad and I was the only girl and I *really* worked very hard. I never went to bed before one in the morning. There was a Swiss student there studying spinning and on Saturdays we would have lunch together and sit until three over our coffee and then go back to our lodgings and I worked until one on Saturday nights. Sundays I was allowed to stay in bed until 10 but I had to start work at 11.'[14]

As the end of the academic year approached, she asked to be entered for the Textile Industry's City and Guilds examination in weaving mechanisms. The college administration hesitated, for it was considered unlikely that anyone could pass without the preparation which the three-year course provided. However, she persevered, and for her long and enthusiastic hours of study in the previous nine months was rewarded with a second class pass.

12   Coleman, *op cit* p39.
13   Marianne Straub has outlined 12 basic types of multi-layered cloths in her book *Handweaving and Cloth Design*, Pelham Books, 1977, pp100–128.
14   Taped interview (no 1) with Marianne Straub, *op cit.*

Design in a handweaver's studio: Gospels

At the completion of the Bradford Technical College course Marianne Straub was invited to work at Ethel Mairet's studio, Gospels (Fig 2.1). As was true throughout her career, the opportunity arose through a combination of friendship and Marianne Straub's willingness to tackle any weaving challenge, even at a moment's notice. In this case the moment came during the long Whitsun weekend of 1933, when she was invited to Gospels by Bianca Fischer, a colleague from the Zurich art school. Ethel Mairet was leaving for Scandinavia the next day, to be joined three days later by one of her ex-assistants at Gospels, Margery Kendon. The latter was a very skilled spinner and had woven on the plain warps preferred at that time by Mrs Mairet. Thus when Margery Kendon complained that she had nothing special to wear to Copenhagen, Marianne Straub volunteered to weave a textured cloth

Fig 2.1 The exterior of Gospels, Ditchling, built by Ethel Mairet 1919–20, showing the windows to the double-height weaving room.

(similar to a honeycomb), beginning the warp immediately and finishing the work the following morning. Martel Biller, a dressmaker at Gospels, made it up into a blouse and it was duly noticed by Ethel Mairet when Margery Kendon arrived. Mrs Mairet's sensitive eye was clearly delighted with this departure from the Gospel's style, for when Bianca Fischer announced her intention to return to Switzerland in July of that year, she requested the friend '. . . who had woven the cloth for the blouse' as a replacement.

For Marianne Straub it was a brief return to the non-industrial weaving of her art school days, and she immersed herself in weaving, spinning and dyeing. The latter two she had never attempted before, nor was she to have the opportunity to continue dyeing in her work after leaving Gospels. However, the sensitivity to colour which Marianne Straub was to later demonstrate in her blending of wool for the Welsh mills and her selection of palettes for Helios (especially the madder-red shades) showed the influence of her enthusiasm for the Gospels dye-house. Mrs Mairet obtained hand-spun silks through her contacts in India and she and Elizabeth Peacock had purchased a large amount of handspun cotton at the Empire Exhibition at Wembley in 1924. Marianne Straub was struck with '. . . all the beautiful yarns such as I'd never seen before.' She found it '. . . most inspiring to really get going on those lovely colours and . . . it was an enormous stimulus in my work, which had been much more designing cloths.'[1] And it was in designing on the loom that Marianne Straub's influence was to be felt.

When Marianne Straub arrived at Gospels the output typically consisted in the main of plain weave cloth, some with the addition of crammed stripes and the typical Scandinavian 'M's and O's' effect (Fig 2.2) achieved through a weft distorting cloth construction. 'All the looms there were 4-shaft looms and one never did anything more than what one could do within the range of those 4-shaft looms. That was perfectly right. All the fabrics had the vitality, the quality and the sparkle that you find in much more highly developed fabrics.'[2] But Bianca Fischer, who had been given the task of setting up the newly acquired 8-shaft countermarch loom, had already extended the range of cloths made in the workshop. The great variety of traditional Gospels plain woven silks in stripes and checks were very striking, and these were used primarily as dress material, shawls or scarves. The distorted weave effect was mainly used for cotton fabrics, curtains, cushion covers etc, while for woollen cloths the weavers returned to plain weave. With the exception of a woollen warp

yarn, most yarns used at Gospels at that time were hand spun, giving the cloths a beautiful texture and subtle handle. All yarns were dyed with natural dyes, though Ethel Mairet had become interested in chemical dyeing, stimulated by a young dye-chemist, Albert Riefstaal, from ICI Manchester, who worked for a few days at Gospels — demonstrating — shortly before Marianne Straub's arrival.

Marianne Straub never worked on the existing warps, preferring to make her own. Her first warp caused considerable comment, containing seven different handspun yarns and made more difficult to put on the loom because Gospels had no raddle (a coarse reed used to spread the warp to the correct width). Despite Mrs Mariet's initial scepticism about weavers with a technical college training, Marianne Straub was soon accepted and quickly began to add her own ideas to the range of cloths being produced at Gospels. She also convinced Mrs Mariet of the benefits of a technical training, and afterwards many students at Gospels were to have this recommended to them.[3]

One weave which Marianne Straub introduced to Gospels late in 1933 was the doublecloth, which has two surfaces of plain or figured construction which share a given proportion of threads interchanged at intervals to bind the

CRAFT STUDY CENTRE. BATH

Fig 2.2 Gospels interior, c1928.

1 Taped interview (no 1) with Marianne Straub, *op cit.*
2 Cox, Peter (ed) *op cit,* p33. Marianne Straub's lecture was given on Saturday, 19 July 1952. In subsequent discussion (*ibid* p112) she commented 'About Mrs Mairet's workshop, I would not consider that a small scale industry at all; in fact, it is probably the most individual workshop there ever was. If someone comes, likes a piece of stuff and wants 7 yards when Mrs Mairet has only got 4, nothing on earth would make her move to make those 7 yards if she didn't feel like it . . .'
3 Joyce Griffiths, apprentice at Gospels from September 1934 to September 1935, had previously attended the Slade School of Art and she helped convince Ethel Mairet of the benefits of *art school* training.

fabric. The simplest form of doublecloth has both horizontal and vertical threads interchanged at intervals to bind the fabric. According to the size of yarn used, the cloth can be thick or thin. More complex weaves vary the relationship of back cloth to face cloth, restrict the exchange to vertical or horizontal threads only, or increase the number of 'cloths' involved to three or more. (At Warners Marianne Straub produced a five-layer doublecloth of carbon fibre, which was so constructed for extreme rigidity.)

Because everyone working at Gospels was accustomed to weaving on 4-shaft looms, the first doublecloths were made with horizontal warp

Fig 2.3 Doublecloths woven by Marianne Straub at Gospels, 1933–34.

exchanges only, giving a horizontal striped design. Textured effects were obtainable too, by combining cloths of very different character (Fig 2.3). One such cloth was inspired by a Tibetan padded jacket. Marianne Straub reduced the jacket's outer cloth, filling and lining into one cloth made up of alternate black and white cotton warp ends, the weft of the face cloth being handspun blue cotton and of the back cloth, a very thick soft woollen yarn. At intervals of about $\frac{1}{2}$ inch a fine, dark blue, cotton pick stitched the two cloths together. Double weft cloths were another variation which she successfully developed for Gospels. Typical of this type were cloths which were made with an undyed Eri silk warp and a weft with two picks of dyed Eri silk for the face alternating with one pick of soft, loosely spun undyed Southdown fleece for the back of the cloth. Such cloth combined the subdued sheen of the Eri silk and the softness of the wool, creating a subtly beautiful, warm fabric, ideal for garments. The quality of the handspun wools and the beauty of the vegetable-dyed silks were a great delight for Marianne Straub and her work at Gospels consistently showed them to their best advantage.

The second innovation she brought to Mariet's studio was the use of 'S' and 'Z' twist effects and therefore directly reflects the impact of her opportunity to spin while at Gospels. Traditional Scottish tweeds employ one twist in the warp and the opposite in the weft, producing a much more pronounced twill as a result of the conflicting tensions. Its use had diminished as high-speed, low-cost production became more important, for it required two stocks of yarns kept carefully apart. In crepe weaving this problem was simplified, for crepe, which employs alternating 'S' and 'Z' twisted yarns in both warp and weft, is piece dyed, so that one twist can be undyed and the other tinted to distinguish them during weaving. However, most manufacturers disliked mixing yarn twists in one cloth so that by the 1930s it was seldom used by industry. For the handweaver the extra time (and therefore cost) was minimal, making it an ideal special effect with no machine-made equivalent.

Marianne Straub's use of the 'S' and 'Z' twists differed from the Scottish twill and crepe weave in that she exploited it for colour effect rather than for texture. The cloth she introduced to Gospels consisted of a weft of 'S' and 'Z' twists of yarns plied with at least two colours. When woven with a uniform warp this produced a pattern of horizontal stripes created by the small diagonals visible within the weft yarn (Fig 2.4). The grouping of yarns in the weft determined the pattern. The first 'S/Z' twist cloth was produced

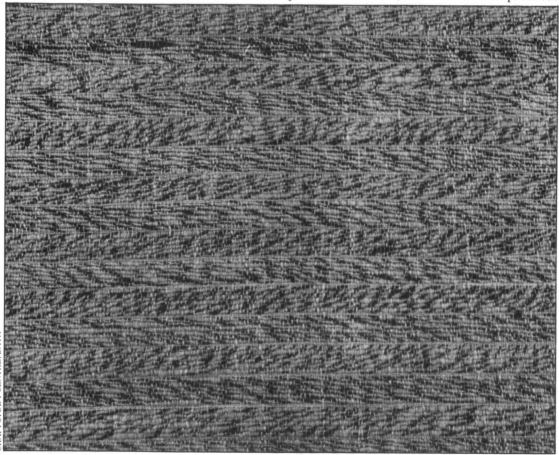

Fig 2.4 Plain weave dress fabric employing alternate S/Z twists in hand-spun undyed Eri silk, Southdown wool and black cotton, designed and woven by Marianne Straub in 1936. (CSC T.74.149.)

after Marianne Straub left Gospels, one Sunday on a weekend visit from Wales in 1936, while 'just playing about' twisting some available hand-spun undyed Southdown yarn with some dark brown Eri silk. Marianne Straub was then working at Holywell Mill in North Wales, but despite their twisting frame with separate spindles which could be altered to produce a reverse twist, she had little chance to exploit twist effect in the Welsh woollens. However, such cloths continued to be woven at Gospels long after 1936. Variations of Marianne Straub's doublecloths also continued to be made at Gospels for a number of years. Both types of cloth, together with the traditional Gospels weaves, were exhibited and sold at the annual Red Rose Guild exhibitions in

CRAFT STUDY CENTRE. BATH

Fig 2.5 Jacket woven and made in 1939 for Edith Solomon. The weave, with a spaced reeding effect which exploits the contrast of thick undyed wool and fine dyed and undyed cotton, was developed by Marianne Straub. (CSC T.74.11.)

Manchester, the Three Shields Gallery and Little Gallery in London, and, from 1935, in Ethel Mariet's shop in Brighton. Garments were made up both at Gospels and through the Brighton shop, including jackets of the cloths which Marianne Straub designed (Fig 2.5).[4]

Ethel Mairet's enthusiasm for new ideas was never dulled by her lack of precise understanding of techniques, nor was she against new fibres. She used Cellophane, and welcomed the fibro (rayon staple) which Marianne Straub secured in Wales and sent to Gospels for spinning just before the war. Despite Ethel Mairet's great influence in the revival of hand spinning and dyeing, she was not a traditionalist and thus produced an atmosphere at Gospels which not only fostered creative weaving but also forged life-long friendships. Although Marianne Straub was at Gospels for less than a year, she continued to be a weekend guest on a regular basis until 1937. Joyce Griffiths (née Winters) was an apprentice from September 1934 to September 1935 and recalls that 'Marianne was always coming down and she taught me how to analyse a

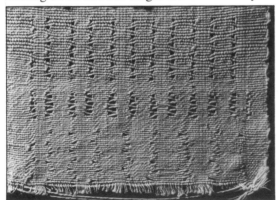

Fig 2.6 Experiment in coarse cotton using a hand-manipulated weave characteristic of Spain. Woven by Marianne Straub at Gospels in November 1943.

fabric, which we should *never* have found out'.[5] In 1935 Mrs Mairet became ill from overwork and Margery Kendon took over the management of Gospels. During this period Marianne Straub helped with design in the workshop, which Margery Kendon believes did much to relieve Mrs Mairet's stress and speed her recovery.[6] Thereafter Marianne Straub visited frequently to the end of Mrs Mairet's life in 1952. During an extended stay in the winter of 1943–44 to recover from the effects of living in the damp Lancashire climate, Marianne Straub designed in the morning for Helios and in the afternoon for Gospels (Fig 2.6). Her work for Gospels during her six months' residence was of a light, open character, using spaced warps or reeding techniques to exploit the juxtaposition of plain and fancy cotton yarns.

As a result of her regular attendance at Gospels, she is often most closely associated with the innovations which characterised the change in the studio's work in the middle years of the 1930s. However, 28 Europeans assisted at Gospels; some came as short-term students, others as cooks or dress-makers. The eight who worked in the weaving room were largely responsible for introducing the more open and complex weaves developed in the studio in the 1930s. Bianca Fischer (née Wassmuth) is credited with the greater textural quality of the cloths. One of the two 8-shaft countermarch looms was set up for Leno weaves by Leanore Maas[7] just before the war, while Dora Schiemann introduced a loop technique which resulted in loosely

4   At least two of these garments survive: T.34–1971 Victoria & Albert Museum and T.74.11 Craft Study Centre, Bath, both made for Edith Soloman 1939.

5   Interview of Joyce Griffiths by Margot Coatts, 14 January 1982, p2.

6   Correspondence from Joyce Griffiths, 3 October 1983.

7   Interview of Marianne Straub by Margot Coatts, 16 May 1982, p8.

woven, almost 'frothy' shawls and stoles. Apart from the two weaves already mentioned, Marianne Straub also experimented with spaced warps, open and float weaves and yarns in unexpected combinations (Fig 2.7).

Margery Kendon, Gospel's apprentice from 1927 to 1929 and designer/weaver from 1933 to 1935, saw Bianca Fischer's artistry and Marianne Straub's technical knowledge as the important factors:

'... between them they revived Gospels at that period, with patterns that they made up — not out of a book... they gave the material a three-dimensional quality which it hadn't had at all.'[8]

Some who had known Gospels before the introduction of the more complex cloths mourned the passing of the predominance of plain cloths which were such effective foils for the beauty of the handspun, hand-dyed yarns. Marianne Straub herself was aware of the changes brought about by the Europeans and in later years came

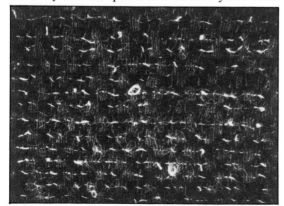

Fig 2.7 *Woollen cloth including Chinese wool with loops created by differential shrinkage of yarn. Designed by Marianne Straub at Gospels, 1943–44 with yarn obtained from Professor Barker, University of Peking.*

to question the value of the contribution made by the German, Swiss and Scandinavian weavers, which did so much to alter the 'handwriting' of Mrs Mairet's earlier Gospels style and she often wonders what would have developed had Mrs Mairet continued undisturbed.

However, Ethel Mairet was a great admirer of Gropius and enthusiastic about Bauhaus ideas being explored at Gospels. She was also one of the first 20th century British weavers to visit Scandinavia, and was impressed by the wide acceptance of weaving as a *modern* craft. Marianne Straub particularly appreciated that 'She loved change and the more adventurous the better; she didn't reject anying *ever*. If you came out with new ideas she was delighted.' Although Ethel Mairet did bring back pieces from her travels and ask others to interpret them, she only asked Marianne Straub once, and otherwise '... she was much, much keener that one should come up with new ideas. That in a way was the fascinating thing.'[9] As had been true at the art school in Zurich, at Gospels Marianne Straub was encouraged always to look forward. She had complete freedom in her work because Ethel Mairet knew less of the technical side of weaving. In addition, while developing a new construction, the practical issue of costing was never discussed — there were no restrictions on the yarns and no requests to produce lengths to a certain price.

The rapport which existed between Ethel Mairet and Marianne Straub was also in part due to Ethel Mairet's increasing belief that standards in industry could be raised by the production of hand-woven prototypes. She first encountered a weaver working thus in 1933 when she met Elsa Gullberry in Stockholm and was greatly impressed.[10] She was no doubt further convinced by Marianne Straub's subsequent success in the Welsh mills. Moreover, Mrs Mairet's love of innovation meant that she gave full rein to anyone who was '... up with the modern things, and so she took to Marianne as a textile designer... her *own* ways practically faded out.'[11] Further, both spoke German, which proved particularly useful on their travels in Europe.

Marianne Straub accompanied Mrs Mairet on three European trips, the first to Finland in 1936. The photographs which record these trips were taken by Marianne Straub (Fig 2.8), who also dealt with all the travel arrangements and accounts. These occasions were often a source of ideas for Mrs Mairet, who would collect objects and textiles to bring back to Gospels, many to sell in her shop. The 'M's and O's' pattern which was frequently used at Gospels was derived from

Fig 2.8 Finland, 1936; photograph by Marianne Straub.

textiles seen on an earlier trip to Scandinavia. Marianne Straub recalls that the trip to Finland had a definite influence on her own work:

'In general my ideas are not based on textiles I have seen, due probably to some extent to the fact that I had been taught by an ex-Bauhaus designer. After the First World War there was this urge for new thinking, new techniques, new designs. It was not done to borrow from the past and other cultures. Though looking back over the twenties I realise that, in the field of fine art, African and Eastern art was already showing its influence. However, in Finland I found textile designs which related to my own thinking, and I was aware that they influenced some of my subsequent designs. I think Mrs Mairet was less influenced because weave constructions were not so easily readable for her.'[12]

Throughout their travels Ethel Mairet kept detailed diaries, which indicate that they devoted large amounts of time to looking at local crafts, architecture, museums and exhibitions, visiting friends at the same time. They made acquaintance with like-minded people whenever possible and, on the 1936 trip to Finland met Alvar Aalto, then designing the Finnish Pavilion for the *Art et Technique* exhibition to be held in Paris the following year. They made four visits to Stockmans, a large store in Helsinki which devoted an entire floor to modern crafts and which Ethel

8   Interview of Margery Kendon by Margot Coatts, 13 January 1982, p8.

9   Taped interview (no 1) with Marianne Straub, *op cit.*

10 Coatts, Margot, *A Weaver's Life: Ethel Mairet 1872—1952*, Crafts Council, London 1983, p89.

11 Interview of Hilary Bourne by Margot Coatts, 15 January 1982, p2.

12 Interview of Marianne Straub by Margot Coatts, *op cit* p12; edited by Marianne Straub.

Mairet had discovered on a previous trip. Here they had a long talk with Mrs Greta Nordlin-Sittnikow, a weaver in charge of the crafts department. Ethel Mairet noted raffia bags and 'good cheap pottery',[13] some of which she purchased.

In 1937 they travelled to Paris to see the *Art et Technique* exhibition, where Marianne Straub found the Portuguese and Finnish pavilions the most interesting. The British Pavilion had been organised by Frank Pick's Council for Art and Industry and included Welsh woollens Marianne Straub had designed. Four members of the Zurich *Kunstgewerbeschule* staff were also in Paris for the same purpose, among them Heinz Otto Hürlimann. This was to be only a brief trip for Ethel Mairet, but Marianne Straub stayed on with her Swiss friends.

The final trip they made was the following year, travelling to Finland, Germany, and Switzerland. By 1938 Ethel Mairet had become more interested in teaching, and was in the process of writing *Hand-Weaving Today,* in which she expressed concern over the lack both of a modern

concept of crafts in relation to machinery and the proper training schools to advance such concepts in England. Not surprisingly, more time was therefore given to visits to schools and workshops. They stopped in Copenhagen and Helsinki, visiting a spinning factory at nearby Ekenäs (Fig 2.9). They next flew to Viipuri, which they had visited in 1936, but this time went on by train to Lake Lagoda to see the workshop of Greta Skogster, a weaver of furnishing fabrics very highly regarded in Finland. From Finland they journeyed through Stettin to Berlin, going immediately to the Ausstellung, an international crafts exhibition.

All of the next day was spent at the *Textile und Modefachschule,* about which Ethel Mairet recorded six enthusiastic pages. As at the *Kunstgewerbeschule* in Zurich which they were to visit the following week, all staff members worked part-time and in the weaving school there was a strong emphasis on artificial materials. Similarly, they visited both the German and Swiss equivalent of the Rural Industries Bureau shop and in the Berlin shop bought two rag rugs. They also visited the *Deutsche Werkstätten* in Berlin and met Margaret Leischner, a Bauhaus trained 'youngish enthusiastic weaver' with a '... very decided character — knows nothing about the actual materials — uses what she wants to express her ideas in textiles.'[14] Margaret Leischner made prototypes for the *Deutsche Werkstätten* and among the materials she used were black Cellophane, synthetic horsehair and thick spun rayon. They also saw Cellophane material by Fraulein Fichard at Dora Sheimann's (a former Gospels helper) but, although Ethel Mairet left Berlin with a cellophane supplier's address, it was in Switzerland that she saw the material used to her satisfaction. Before leaving Berlin they met Dr Marie Schuette, the past curator of the Grassi Museum in Leipzig and an expert on lace. They also went to the *Völkerkunst*

CRAFT STUDY CENTRE, BATH

Fig 2.9 Ethel Mairet (left) and Marianne Straub (right) on their second trip to Finland in 1938, while at Ekenäs with Mrs Boije and Miss Brueneck. Photograph by Gerd Bergerson.

Museum which held a large, fine collection of Peruvian textiles. Dr Schuette was later to visit the Whitworth Art Gallery in Manchester and maintained contact with Margaret Pilkington and Marianne Straub.

In Switzerland they met Herr Fritz Ikle, whose family was noted for their collection of textiles, and with whom they had a 'very interesting conversation' on ikats and Peruvian textiles. Their hosts in Switzerland were Heinz Otto Hürlimann and the Straubs; Hürlimann took them to the art school and his studio. Ethel Mairet was enthusiastic about his use of cellophane and it was one of his cellophane pieces which she purchased from the *Wohnbedarf,* a 'good and interesting shop' which also sold Aalto chairs covered 'exactly right' with woven stuff from North Africa. While in Zurich they also visited Gunta Stöltz's studio. She had also trained at the Bauhaus, and later was senior weave tutor there. For a short period she and Hürlimann shared a studio, and the work she was producing in Zurich showed '. . . a real understanding of materials and colour' which was 'somewhat limited by the impending war in Europe.'[15] Although Ethel Mairet noted the fortifications along the German/Swiss border, she optimistically made plans in both Berlin and Zurich to return the next year. She was, in fact, never to travel outside Britain again, although Marianne Straub returned to Switzerland the following year for the Swiss national exhibition, held every 25 years. By then it was clear that war was imminent. Her family knew it would be a long time before she would return again, but they could hardly have guessed that it would be seven years.

Although much has been said regarding Marianne Straub's contribution to Gospels, the influence of Ethel Mairet on *her* cannot be underestimated. The continued enthusiasm for her work, the open door at Gospels, with its wide ranging contacts, the love of experiment, and the European travels, all laid the foundation for increasing confidence Marianne Straub found in herself. Joyce Griffiths described her as the daughter of the house, recalling that, 'Mrs Mairet was obviously very proud of her and she often said "You should have seen her when she came from Bradford and look at her now!"' (Fig 2.10)[16]

Such support was crucial to the young Swiss weaver, who repaid Mrs Mairet by becoming 'all that a Gospels weaver should be.'[17] Gospels also provided Marianne Straub with her introduction to the English Arts and Crafts tradition, in which Mrs Mairet had been deeply immersed.[18] There

JOHN PIPER

Fig 2.10 Outside Gospels in the mid-1930s (left to right) Miss Flavin, Margery Kendon, Hilde Biller, Karen Jorgensen and Marianne Straub.

13 Ethel Mairet Travel Journal, 24 June–12 July 1936, p2, Craft Study Centre, Bath.
14 Ethel Mairet Travel Journal 'Germany', 20–25 June 1938, p17, Craft Study Centre, Bath.
15 Ethel Mairet Travel Journal 'Switzerland', *op cit* p14 and p16.
16 Correspondence from Joyce Griffiths, 3 October 1983.
17 *Ibid.*
18 See Coatts, Margot, *A Weaver's Life, op cit* pp11–33.

were also other craftsmen nearby — Elizabeth Peacock, Eric Gill, Edward Johnston and Douglas Pepler — whom Marianne Straub came to know.

Against the background of Gospels must also be set another life-long friendship. Marianne Straub never met Margaret Pilkington during her first nine months at Gospels, but knew that she had founded the Red Rose Guild (RRG) and annually organised their exhibition of craftsmen's work in Manchester, where she was also (from 1936) Honorary Director of the Whitworth Art Gallery. During the 1930s she lent considerable financial and moral support to Gospels, and among her purchases was a dress material by Marianne Straub. Ethel Mairet often spoke of Margaret Pilkington, and regarded the Red Rose exhibition as her best outlet for sale of Gospels' work. Marianne Straub visited the RRG exhibition while working in Wales, but missed meeting Margaret Pilkington. It was not until 1937 that they eventually met, when Marianne Straub was in Sir Thomas Barlow's office on her way to begin work at Bolton and Margaret Pilkington happened to come in to discuss some Whitworth gallery matters. They already had a great deal in common — particularly their interest in weaving and in Gospels. In addition Margaret Pilkington was a great friend of Sir Thomas's.

Margaret Pilkington became the chief trustee of Gospels upon Ethel Mairet's death in 1952 and planned the future of Gospels in the hope that J.S. Southern or Marianne Straub would carry it on. Southern had also been a frequent visitor to Gospels during the 1940s but at the time of Ethel Mairet's death was in Nigeria, working through the British government to revive the local weaving. Marianne Straub preferred to remain an industrial designer. With further financial support from Margaret Pilkington a small company was formed which maintained Gospels for four years until Southern could take charge. In the interim the contents of the house were put into chests, the books put away, the workshop closed and the remainder of the house let to non-weavers. When Southern returned he found Gospels difficult to run alone, and Margaret Pilkington had to continue her financial support. The committee (Margaret Pilkington; Marianne Straub; Stopford Jacks; Mr Ginett, a solicitor; and later Ann Bristol, then teaching at the Central School) had once again to consider the future of Gospels. Gospels was part of Margaret Pilkington's estate, and her family became concerned about the consequences should death duties have to be paid on it. The decision was taken to sell Gospels to a craftsman sympathetic to the work that had been carried out there, and in due course it was sold to Tadek Beutlick and Margaret Pilkington's investment in the house was repaid. He remained at Gospels until 1970, when he moved to Spain.

The contents of Gospels, which had been sorted by Marianne Straub with the aid of Margery Kendon and Joan Partridge, were stored until a home could be found for them. The need for a crafts study centre was obvious and discussion began between Henry Hammond, Christine Lefroy, Muriel Rose, Marianne Straub and Robin Tanner regarding how best to use Ethel Mairet's collection and other 20th century craft material. After 12 years of planning, the Crafts Study Centre was opened at the Holborn and Menstrie Museum in Bath in 1977 (Fig 2.11). Marianne Straub became one of the 11 trustees of the Crafts Centre, which now holds examples of the work of over 80 craftsmen, including the furniture, pottery, books, textile collection and samples from Gospels, thus retaining her links with Gospels to this day.

Fig 2.11 The Craft Study Centre collection holds the majority of surviving Gospels samples. This piece by Marianne Straub (in a private collection) is typical of the small size of many (10 × 15 cm).

Design for rural industry: Wales

During her months at Gospels Marianne Straub had been offered a job at the weaving school in Askov, Denmark. Ethel Mairet also discussed with her the possibility that they might be invited to design for the mill at Dartington Hall. However, at the same time the Rural Industries Bureau (RIB) were seeking a weaver to act as a consultant designer to the mills in Wales, and thus in March 1934 Marianne Straub began her wanderings which were to take her, over the course of three years, to many of the 72 Welsh mills then in operation. To understand the task Marianne Straub undertook, it is necessary to briefly outline the developments which created the industry as she met it in the 1930s.

The manufacture of woollens was long established in Wales, although it had never attained the stable position within the Welsh economy as had weaving in Yorkshire and Lancashire. The story of the rise and decline of Welsh textile manufacture is complex, as prosperity shifted from one part of the country to another. In the early 19th century Montgomeryshire, followed by Merioneth, were the leading counties. Whereas a too-rapid and too-late over-expansion produced a spectacular decline during the 1870s and 1880s in Montgomeryshire's flannel mills, Merioneth's mills gradually lost their export market for webs (a hard tough plain white cloth used for clothing soldiers and North American slaves) and with little capital investment gradually returned to the traditional practice of processing wool for the farming population of the surrounding countryside.

By 1900 both these areas had ceased production on any scale, having been superseded by the Western Welsh counties in the last quarter of the 19th century (Fig 3.1). Here, particularly in the Teifi valley of Carmarthenshire, new mills were built next to good road and rail facilities to take their products — shirtings, flannel, tweed and blankets — to their wholesale markets. Many manufacturers of flannel also sent their shirting cloth to the colliery districts, concentrated in South Wales. The miners provided a large, steady demand for the sturdy flannel shirtings, which, in their design, demonstrated the conversion from hand to power looms which accompanied the growth of the Western Wales textile industry. The hand-woven flannel shirtings were traditionally checked, but the introduction of the powerlom with only one shuttle, limited the pattern to the warp, producing stripes.

Fig 3.1 Alltcafan Mill, Pentre-Cwrt, Camarthen, c1935.

By the early 20th century the much reduced woollen industry remained of the Merioneth type: utilising local wool either purchased or exchanged for finished goods, employing a handful of people (often a family who farmed or practised another craft for part of the year), and selling any surplus goods through local retail outlets such as markets and fairs. The only exceptions to this pattern were the large mills in the Western counties, three mills in Llangollen and one mill in Holywell, North Wales. The cloths manufactured in the rural mills were heavy tweeds, blankets, bedcovers, flannels and knitting yarns. Some also made flannels for the South Wales market. The introduction of powerlooms into the larger factories contributed to the decline of rural mills, which continued steadily until 1914.

During the First World War the woollen industry had a temporary reprieve due to contracts from the War Office and the Romanian Government for innumerable blankets and vast amounts of flannel and other material for uniforms. The profits went largely to the manufacturers in West Wales, few of whom invested it in capital equipment, continuing instead to use machinery already at least 30 (and as much as 60) years old. When the war ended the manufacturers were faced with three problems. First, a surplus of government stock was put into the open market, forcing mill owners to cut prices and costs and creating both unemployment at the mills and severe hardship among the farmers, who saw the price of their wool fall from 54 pence (per pound) in 1919 to 7¾ pence in 1922. Second, the miners' strike in South Wales in 1921 largely destroyed the main market for the traditional textiles of both the large and small mills in West and South Wales. Finally, fashions changed. Flannel was little used for clothing by the 1920s, for knitted underwear was more attractive. In addition, unions and cotton flannel-

ettes offered a cheaper substitute, and these cloths were widely available by mail order or through local shops, as were ready-made suits. As the latter became increasingly fashionable, so the trade in Welsh homespuns and tweeds declined, and with these the village tailors.

The textile manufacturers in Western Wales were unable to meet the challenge of these changing circumstances and in one village alone 21 factories closed in the 1920s.[1] Conditions were such that the University of Wales commissioned a report by W.P. Crankshaw, who began his study in 1925 and concluded it in 1927. The Crankshaw report was undertaken with practical and financial support from the RIB and its objective was to determine the best use of a small fund set aside by the University of Wales for the assistance of the Welsh textile industry. Crankshaw concluded that:

'. . . whilst I have frequently expressed my admiration of these fine old craftsmen, it should be said that their skill as workers is somewhat discounted by their strict adherence to traditional methods and fabrics. They generally fail to achieve excellence through inability to break away from these traditional ideas and to adapt themselves to modern circumstances and materials.'[2]

He believed that the major cause of the industry's decline was the change in fashion that almost eliminated demand. The new fashions contributed to the penetration of Yorkshire's woollens and Lancashire's softer, less expensive cloths. The farmers' preference for such fabrics meant that they sold their wool crop at a fair and

1   Jenkins, J. Geraint, *The Welsh Woollen Industry,* National Museum of Wales, Welsh Folk Museum, Cardiff, 1969, p281.

2   Crankshaw, W.P., *Report on a survey of the Welsh woollen industry made on behalf of the University of Wales,* 1927, p15.

were paid in currency rather than converting their wool to cloth and yarn at the local mill.

However there were several reasons why the Welsh textile manufacturers could not attempt to compete directly with the English cloths, namely the location of the mills, the character of the local wool, and the machinery. Many mills were extremely inaccessible, for their location had been determined by the presence of adequate water power supplies. Jenkins, in his comprehensive study, *The Welsh Woollen Industry,* cites two examples:

'The Farthings Hook Mill at Clarbeston Road, Pembrokeshire, was approached from a third-grade road and a visit to it would involve a walk across fields for nearly half a mile, which in rainy weather must have been in the nature of a swamp. The Trewindsor Mill, near Cardigan, which closed in 1963, was located at the bottom of a gorge, and was approached by several footpaths and an extremely steep, mile-long, rutted, cart-track.'[3]

The Welsh wool produced a harder yarn and was generally regarded as of a lower quality than the Yorkshire wool. The quality of the Welsh yarn was further reduced by the condition of the carding machines, through which the wool was processed prior to spinning. Since good cloth requires good yarn, and good yarn must be well carded, Crankshaw had no doubts as to the seriousness of the problem, going so far as to say that 'The very sight of some of the carding engines is enough to drive any well trained carder to commit suicide.' Virtually every carding engine Crankshaw saw required re-clothing. The rest of the machinery was antiquated, since 'knowledge of the introduction of . . . machinery reached the Welsh manufacturer . . . about 50 years after it had taken place in other woollen manufacturing districts'[4] and when finally introduced came in the form of machines discarded by the Yorkshire mills on the installation of modern equipment. The first dobby, widely used elsewhere in the 19th century, was introduced at Llanwrtyd, Brecknockshire in about 1927, only seven years before Marianne Straub began designing in Wales, and the Jacquard, in use in other textile manufactures from about 1816, was never appropriate to the Welsh woollen industry. Even the most complex doublecloths were woven on dobbies. This situation was exacerbated by the fact that there were no competent textile engineers in the region who were capable of repairing the machines, and those who leased mills were loath to replace or repair machines which were not their own.

Nevertheless, Crankshaw believed that, by bringing the carding engines up to standard, 'the position would not be so hopeless'[5] for the remaining machinery was considered adequate for their purpose and the comparatively small total output involved. Although one mill had over 100 powerlooms, the majority in the mid-1920s had less than four and some continued weaving by hand. Thus for the mills to survive, they needed — not new and different machinery — but a new *image* which exploited the existing equipment and the character of the Welsh wools. Crankshaw stressed that this could only be obtained by raising the aesthetic quality of the Welsh textiles.

The first step towards this goal was the creation of a technical advisor to assist in the refurbishing of machines. This role was undertaken by Maldwyn Williams, whose appointment in 1929 was supported by the University of Wales' special fund and a grant from the Development Commission. The second step was the

3 Jenkins, *op cit* p263.
4 Crankshaw, *op cit* p13.
5 *Ibid.*

formation of the Welsh Textiles Association Ltd, in 1931. Its stated aims were:

— to supply technical advice and assistance to manufacturers of Welsh textiles;
— to secure registered trade marks for the products of Welsh mills (finally achieved in 1968, 25 years after the Association disbanded);
— to provide raw materials and patterns;
— to provide an organisation for selling Welsh textiles;
— to set up a dyeing and finishing plant;
— to be responsible for publicity and advertising;
— to encourage the establishment of new mills and stimulate the manufacture of textiles products.[6]

The Association was formed with the support of J. Ruppert Brooke, Director of the Rural Industries Bureau, who realised that, '. . . although technical advice was offered, it was not accepted.'[7] Through the Welsh Textiles Association an effort was made to encourage the small manufacturers to make tweeds and furnishing fabrics, the latter particularly well suited to the 'hard' Welsh wools. However, the small mills were not able to carry out the experiments necessary to produce contemporary fabrics and it was therefore decided to accept the offer of Thomas Waterhouse (the chairman of the Association and Managing Director of Holywell, the largest mill in Wales) to place Holywell's preparing, spinning, weaving and finishing machinery at the disposal of the Association for experimental purposes. The Rural Industries Bureau agreed to fund the appointment of a designer (there were three prior to Marianne Straub) and, through the aid of the Design and Industries Association, contacted Minnie McLeish. For six months, until her departure for India in the autumn of 1932, she paid regular visits to Wales to advise on the production of new tweeds and furnishing fabrics. However, her designs were not a success, for the colours she had to work with were considered 'artistically bad'.[8] It had been decided that, in order to obtain uniform dyes, fast to milling and to light, all dyeing was to be done by contract until output and sales justified setting up a Welsh dyeing and finishing factory for the Association. The resulting colours were 'metallic horrors'.[9] Miss McLeish's successor Gerd Bergersen, persevered, aided by Waterhouse's personal support and Brooke's conviction that the experiment could succeed.[10] By the spring of 1933 they were rewarded with products thought worthy of the textile section of the British Industries Fair (Fig 3.2). Brooke was also able to report that, despite experiments to improve the texture and handle of cloths which had not 'got very far or . . . succeeded very well'[11] (due to the difficulties of working with a yarn blended from Welsh and Shropshire wool), the Bureau had decided to

'. . . make permanent the co-operation of the artist hand loom weaver with the power

6 Jenkins, *op cit* p399.
7 *Report on work of the Rural Industries Bureau 1929–36,* HMSO, 1936, p16.
8 Brooke, J.R.I. 'Fighting Unemployment by Improved Design', *Journal of the Rural Industries Bureau,* Spring 1933, p11.
9 Brooke, J.R.I. 'Survival and Revival: An Experiment in Wales', *Design for Today* May 1933, p21.
10 Brooke was well aware of the problems they faced, saying (*ibid* p22) 'Manufacturers who desire to employ an artist to improve the colour and design of their product will only succeed if they make up their minds to forget what they imagine they know, and place their craftsmen at the service of the artist they employ. Preconceived notions of what is good design founded on the past successes of an industry are ... the greatest stumbling-blocks to the production of new fabrics designed to satisfy a new standard of taste, which the manufacturer and his present advisors may not have recognised.'
11 Brooke, J.R.I. 'Fighting Unemployment . . .' *op cit* p11.

loom producer, that some day fabrics may be produced by *ci-devant* flannel manufacturers worthy to be shown beside the creations of the great French designers.'[12]

He was not to know that, within two years, Welsh textiles were to achieve the standard he dreamed of, for he died in 1934.

Gerd Bergersen, a Norwegian hand loom weaver, remained a designer at Holywell for 18 months. For a short period she was preceded by Margery Kendon, who was invited to work in Wales at the suggestion of Ethel Mairet. Margery Kendon had started her own workshop in Midhurst after leaving Gospels in 1930 and found Wales extremely interesting, but '. . . realised at once that I didn't want to work with machinery, but I liked the human beings so much.' She recalls that Brooke, 'who came of a Yorkshire firm that wove the uniforms of the porters of the Bank of England — beautiful worsteds . . . had the Welsh mills very much at heart, and the

Fig 3.2 Holywell tweeds by Gerd Bergersen and Marianne Straub, 1935. These cloths sold for 10–14/– a yard at 54" wide and 15–18/– a yard at 70" wide.

THE ARCHITECTURAL REVIEW

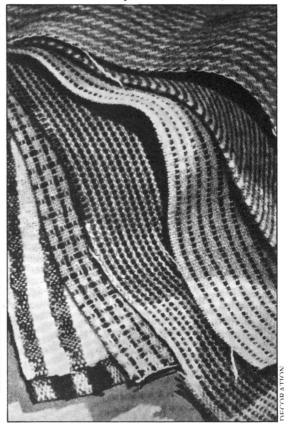

DECORATION

Fig 3.3 Welsh tweeds by Margery Kendon, c1932.

weaving.'[13] He and Mrs Mairet decided that the solution was further training for Margery Kendon, and thus she spent several months at the weaving school in Askov, Denmark, teaching spinning in return for weaving tuition. It was on this trip in 1933 that Margery Kendon wore the blouse Marianne Straub had woven the cloth for. However, the plot failed: 'I came home at the end of 1933, Brooke took me out to lunch and said "Look . . ." and I said, "No, I really can't design for the Welsh mills".'[14]

However, a few cloths were produced to her initial designs (Fig 3.3) and, together with Gerd Bergersen, the two weavers laid the foundation of better design in the Welsh textile manufacture, creating cloths which, through the efforts of the Welsh Textile Association and Maldwyn Williams, were not only exhibited, but illustrated in furnishing journals. Samples were sent to London for comment prior to production and through the RIB were shown to wholesalers, dressmakers and 'persons of taste and discernment.'[15] Ethel Mairet was obviously among those consulted. She also contributed an article to the RIB Journal in the spring of 1932[16] and, when Gerd Bergersen left to take a weaving position in Yorkshire, she was again consulted. She suggested that they appoint Marianne Straub.

There is a natural link between the ideas Marianne Straub developed at Gospels and those that she put into production in Wales between 1934 and 1937, although in many cases the influence is derivative, rather than direct. This is perhaps most obvious in the dyeing and spinning at the mills. Since the formation of the Wool Trading Board in 1950, most Welsh mills have been forced to purchase their yarns from outside sources, most typically Yorkshire, so that they have lost control of the 'ingredients' of their cloths. In the 1930s each Welsh cloth retained its own character, derived from the traditional practices of the mills. Wool was dyed in the fleece

and, although chemically dyed, the mixing of colours during carding offered very subtle shadings which could give each fabric a personality unique to itself. Marianne Straub exploited this process, through which she was able to control the final colour by hand carding and spinning the prototype yarns (Fig 3.4). It was during her years in Wales that the mills began to spin knitting yarns and weave tweeds and flannels to match, a combination which was to prove extremely successful.

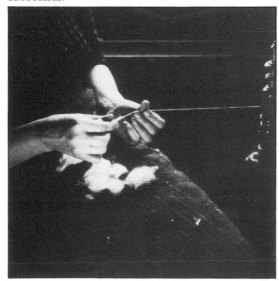

Fig 3.4 Marianne Straub spinning in a madder-dyed Welsh flannel apron, used by the Welsh because they believed the madder counteracted rheumatism.

12   *Ibid.*
13   Interview of Margery Kendon by Margot Coatts, *op cit* p6.
14   *Ibid* p7.
15   Brooke, J.R.I., 'Fighting Unemployment . . .' *op cit* p11.
16   Mairet, Ethel, 'Handweaving in England' *Journal of the Rural Industries Bureau*, Spring 1932, p5.

On average Marianne Straub designed 100 different cloths each year, and the range of goods produced by the mills remained extremely varied. The mills in Mid and South Wales were known for their coloured blankets and bed-spreads and, to these, Marianne Straub introduced new designs and colourings (Fig 3.5). One mill in Cardiganshire wove tweeds designed by Marianne Straub for the French designer Anny Blatt. These were to be used in conjunction with Madame Blatt's hand-knitted garments and were introduced to buyers (among whom were Jaeger) at a London fashion show. The Blatt knitting yarn was predominantly a light single ply, for which the Welsh tweeds were an excellent foil.

To one of the smallest mills in Pembrokeshire, Marianne Straub introduced the weaving of the Finnish type of Rya rug (Fig 3.6). Woven on the powerloom, the ground pick was introduced mechanically, while the long tufts were intro-

duced by hand. A typical design, which had to be easy to follow, exploited the fact that the tufts were made of eight threads and consisted of rows of tufts composed of brown and white strands. The proportion of white to brown was gradually reduced from 7–1 to 1–7, when the colour order

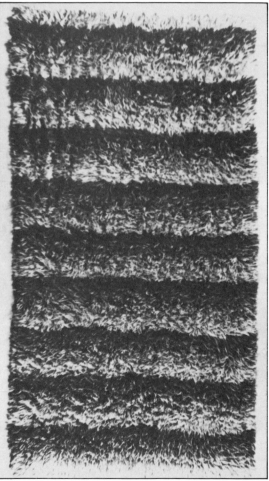

Fig 3.6 Rya rug, one of several designed by Marianne Straub and woven by Mr Morgan at Wallis Mill in Pembrokeshire in 1936.

Fig 3.5 Natural Welsh woollen blanket designed by Marianne Straub for Glanesgaer Mill.

was reversed. The mill, Wallis Factory in Ambleston, was owned by William Morgan, who worked with his son. In 1937 Ethel Mairet visited several Welsh mills with Margaret Pilkington, and at Wallis's she noted a small old carding machine which was '. . . not as effective as others so the resulting thread was interesting and not even' (Fig 3.6). Maldwyn Williams, whose office was located in the Post Office in Newcastle Emlyn, took them to David Davies & Co nearby, where they saw shirt flannel, blankets, knitting yarn and dress tweeds selling at 2/6d a yard (Gordon Russell Ltd at the same date was retailing Welsh furnishing tweeds at 8 to 9 shillings a yard). She also noted elsewhere that single blankets (64 × 90 inches) cost £2 a pair and double blankets (72 × 180 inches) £2 10/– a pair, and in Brecon 'splendid dark natural thick

Fig 3.7 A lightweight Merino cloth with an overcheck of a fine two-ply yarn. One of the many dress cloths produced at Holywell to Marianne Straub's design, c1935.

stuff two yards wide at 7/6d "very thick" and 6/6d "thinner".'[17]

Holywell was the largest of all the mills and required a good deal of the designer's time. Something in the region of 30 new designs were produced annually. These included cloths for ties specially designed for Austin Reed and tweeds for a wide variety of garments made for a number of clients, Hardy Amies among them (Fig 3.7). Holywell also employed a freelance designer with experience in the Yorkshire mills, who designed and got orders for men's suiting tweeds. Marianne Straub developed their range of Welsh doublecloth upholstery fabrics first launched by Gerd Bergensen in 1931–32 (Fig 3.8).[18] The doublecloth fitted well into the scene of Welsh woollen production because doublecloth bedspreads based on traditional damask designs had been produced since the early 1920s. In 1935 Marianne Straub was invited by Dick Russell to bring her range of new upholstery cloths to the London showroom of Gordon Russell Ltd, where Dr Nikolaus Pevsner (later Sir Nikolaus) was present to assist with making the choice of the fabrics they intended to incorporate into their range. These can be seen in the 1936 'Spring Fabrics' catalogue produced by Gordon Russell Ltd (Figs 3.9 & 3.10). Thus began a very useful contact for the Holywell mill[19] and the production of the upholstery cloth range has continued until recently. Heal's made use of her Welsh tweeds on their furniture as early as 1936, and her Holywell tweeds were also offered as lengths by Heal's and later Heal Fabrics Ltd, from the late 1930s well into the

17 Ethel Mariet Travel Journal 'Wales', 23–29 June 1937, p3; Crafts Study Centre, Bath.

18 Marianne Straub also contributed an article 'The Construction of a Double-cloth', to the RIB *Journal,* Summer 1936, pp27–28.

19 Among the tweeds they stocked were a few by Gerd Bergerson which were still being produced in 1935/36.

1950s. Throughout the 1940s and 50s Welsh tweeds were to be found in use by other furniture manufacturers, including H.K. Furniture (Fig 3.11), and they were used extensively by Ernest Race Limited in the 1950s (see Fig 3.17). Marianne Straub relates that in 1965 she passed the new London showrooms of Olivetti and was delighted to see one of her Holywell upholstery cloths on the new furniture.

It is interesting at this point to turn to Pevsner's work *Industrial Art in England,* published in 1937 but largely complete by the end of 1936. In his discussion on the standard of British textiles he cites 'British tweeds, for dress (Munro, Gardiner) as well as for upholstery' among the woven fabrics of 'highest artistic standards [which] would hold their own in Germany, in Sweden, and in France.' He goes further to suggest that '. . . simple texture effects or slight patterns such as indistinct stripes etc, are aes-

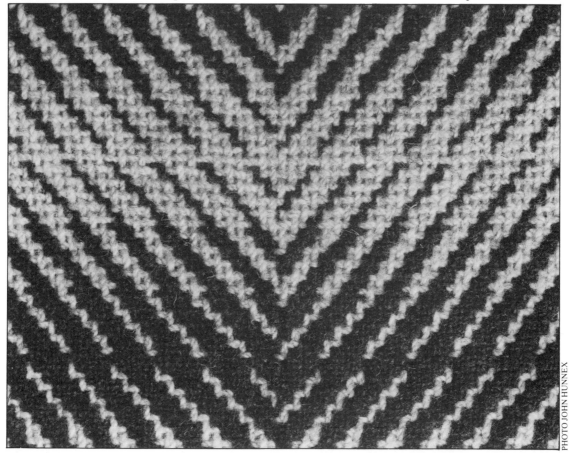

PHOTO JOHN HUNNEX

Fig 3.8 Detail of the Welsh doublecloth used for re-covering furniture at Dolcis in 1937-38.

thetically more successful than the more explicit motifs.'[20] Given that Pevsner was so closely involved with the Russell selection of Welsh tweeds (which he illustrates, see Fig 3.9) and that, additionally, he is known to have visited an exhibition of Welsh textiles in London, it is difficult not to conclude that the so-highly praised fabrics included Welsh cloth made to Marianne Straub's designs.

The 1937 Pevsner report had assessed that

Fig 3.9 Welsh tweeds designed by Marianne Straub exclusive to Gordon Russell Ltd, as seen in their 'Spring Fabrics' brochure of 1936. The fabrics, left, centre and front (GR5221, GR5219 and GR5220) are 54" and retailed at 7/9 to 9/– a yard. The chair covering and right-hand cloth (GR5229 and GR5218) are 70" wide and 11/3 a yard. Pevsner included this among his illustrations in 'Industrial Art in England', 1937.

only 10 per cent of British industrial art had any artistic merit. This sad state of affairs had, from the establishment of the Board of Trade Committee on Art and Education in 1932,[21] led to a proliferation of reports, committees, publications and exhibitions. The successes and failures of these actions are ably discussed by Fiona MacCarthy, who summarises the situation thus:

'Wherever there was progress, this progress could be traced back to just one person fighting the great tide, or as Gordon Russell put it, pushing a tank fanatically uphill. The designers pushing tanks were the Russells, Robert Goodden, Alfred Read, Keith Murray, Enid Marx, Marian Pepler (later Mrs R.D. Russell), Marion Dorn, Marianne Straub — in her 70 Welsh mills — (Serge) Chermayeff, (Wells) Coates, and

Fig 3.10 Kineton suite (no 924) by Gordon Russell, mid 1930s, covered with GR5220 (see Fig 3.9). The cloth is blue, yellow and white on nigger brown.

20 Pevsner, Nikolaus, *An Inquiry into Industrial Art in England*, Cambridge University Press, 1937, p54.
21 Under the Chairmanship of Lord Gorell, after whom the 1932 report is named.

(Raymond) McGrath. As these were mainly architects, design for industry was a spare-time occupation in nine cases out of ten.'[22]

Thus we find Marianne Straub in 1934 — and still in 1951 according to Pevsner's introduction to *Designers in Britain*[23] — an exception to the rule: trained as a textile designer and working as a textile designer. For this reason alone it is natural that her Welsh tweeds would create a favourable impression on those seriously concerned with quality and good design (Fig 3.12).

The very conservative nature of the woollen industry also aided her. Enid Marx recalls that as 'Marianne herself told me later, the first obstacle which she had to overcome was the suspicion of the weavers; they believed that she had been sent to *steal their ideas*.'[24] The tendency among Welsh woollen mill owners to resist change had saved them from many of the attempts to streamline or segregate components of manufacture which had so damaged the quality of production in other industries. Because every mill was largely self-contained, the designer could participate at every stage. Most bought their fleece, sorted it, put it through the devil, dyed it, spun it, wove the cloth and finished it. Not all were receptive to new ideas and Marianne Straub found her understanding of machines invaluable '. . . because if the mill owner said he could not produce the cloth I had suggested . . . I could set the warp up myself, and do some weaving. That soon got them wanting to do it themselves.'[25] Her understanding of the machinery and ability to produce a prototype yarn and cloth which could be exactly duplicated guaranteed that the finished cloth was precisely what she intended. In all,

HK/PHOTO JOHN GAY

Fig 3.11 HK Khyber chair, c1936, covered with Welsh upholstery tweed designed by Marianne Straub and woven at Holywell textile mills.

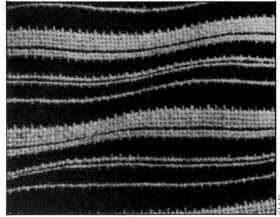

Fig 3.12 A doublecloth upholstery weight fabric by Marianne Straub, one of four Welsh tweeds by Marianne Straub, designed c1935 and still in production 12 years later when it was selected for inclusion in the SIA's first volume of Designers in Britain.

perhaps a dozen mills actively sought her assistance and for these she produced ranges. The remainder she visited to make suggestions.

This was most often undertaken in conjunction with Maldwyn Williams, the technical advisor of the Welsh Mills, who lived in South Wales. Marianne Straub, based at Holywell in North Wales, would join him for their car journeys to mills which were almost inevitably situated down a narrow lane to an unsigned turning. The inaccessibility of the mills was a characteristic which Williams recognised as a serious drawback to the survival of Welsh weaving. Although the RIB financed the advisors they were unable to give any assistance towards promotion. The presence of a London representative, Miss Caddell, slightly eased the isolation of the Welsh mills, but Williams was determined to do more. He thus began to organise exhibitions which were specifically designed to establish new outlets for the Welsh products, beginning in 1933 with participation in the annual exhibition held each February at David Morgan's, a major department store in Cardiff. Undertaken jointly with the Monmouthshire

RCC, these exhibitions were recorded in the RIB Journal, which noted that the 1935, '36 and '37 exhibitions showed higher standards and increased orders. At the invitation of the organisers, Williams staged an exhibition of woollen goods at the Royal Welsh Shows, and later, on two occasions in the 1950s, Marianne Straub was invited to judge the entries for the best textiles. In 1936 she spent the three days of the show demonstrating hand spinning. Gradually displays were included in most of the Welsh agricultural shows and further afield at the Bath and West show and in Barrow Stores in Birmingham. In London exhibitions were held under the auspices of the Welsh Textile Association, who contributed to the British Industries Fairs of 1933–39 (Fig. 3.13). Of the 1934 exhibition, the RIB journal reported:

'The advisory and practical help which has been given to the smaller textile mills throughout Wales has now definitely succeeded in enabling these small producers to put on the market fabrics which, entirely Welsh in material and workmanship, have the essential qualities of modern dress fabrics.'[26]

In 1936 the Welsh Textile Association organised an exhibition for the London Welsh Hall, which '. . . supplied evidence of the remarkable devel-

RURAL INDUSTRIES BUREAU

Fig 3.13 The Rt Hon Lloyd George and Miss Megan Lloyd George at the stand of the Welsh Textile Association Ltd at the British Industries Fair in 1934.

22   MacCarthy, Fiona, *All Things Bright and Beautiful: Design in Britain 1830 to Today,* University of Toronto Press, 1972, p109.

23   Pevsner, Nikolaus, 'A Century of Industrial Design and Designers, 1851–1951', *Designers in Britain,* Allan Wingate, vol 3, 1951, pp178–179.

24   Correspondence from Enid Marx, 17 February 1984. In the same letter she concludes, 'In fact the Welsh hand weaving and some factory weaving today I think can claim that it really owes its existence to Marianne's efforts.'

25   Coleman, *op cit* p40.

26   *Journal of the Rural Industries Bureau,* Spring 1934, p4.

opment in this industry which has taken place during the short space of five years.'[27]

The Welsh woollen manufacturers had the RIB showrooms in London as a further outlet, and received support from the RIB whenever possible. One such occasion was an exhibition of English and Welsh woollens, yarns, fleeces and flaxes displayed in Stockholm in 1934 at the invitation of the *Svenska Hemslöjdsföreningarnas Riksföfbund* (Swedish Rural Industries Bureau) (Fig 3.14). In 1935 Welsh woollens designed by Marianne Straub were included in the first exhibition of spinning, weaving and dyeing organised by the Guild of Weavers, Spinners and Dyers at the Whitechapel Gallery in London.[28] Submissions to international exhibitions followed: in 1937 the British Pavilion (designed by Oliver Hill) at the *Art et Technique* exhibition in Paris had two floors with a connecting ramp; the wall opposite was entirely covered with lengths of Welsh woollens.

The success of the exhibitions in generating sales was welcomed at the mills, but created problems for the public, who were interested in ordering or reordering goods. To deal with such

Fig 3.14 The woollen section of the RIB's exhibit at the exhibition held by the Svenska Hemslöjdsföreningarnas Riksföbund *at Stockholm in 1934.*

inquiries Maldwyn Williams created a mail order business, trading through the Welsh Textile Association. The increased trade through better design and wider exposure had a clear effect on the Welsh woollen industry for, between 1932 and the beginning of the war, only a handful of mills closed. The 'experiment' had produced positive gains. That the excellence of Marianne Straub's Welsh cloths was noticed in spite of the inaccessibility of the mills was clearly in part due to the promotional work of Maldwyn Williams. However, despite the increased exposure the mills received through such efforts, the RIB were uncertain how much approval they could grant such commercial activities. Marianne Straub too, was growing tired of her nomadic life, which had necessitated leaving many of her possessions at Gospels. Both factors prompted her to accept Sir Thomas Barlow's offer in 1937 to join Helios, the newly formed auxiliary company of Barlow & Jones. Maldwyn Williams stayed on until early in 1939, when he and his wife opened the first Welsh craft shop, in Cardiff, remaining technical adviser on a part-time basis only. At the outbreak of war he undertook the rationing of wool in Wales and at the war's end opened his own four loom mill in Velindre, which he ran until 1970.[29]

By 1937, when Marianne Straub left Wales to join Helios, the woollen industry had established its well designed tweeds as part of the vocabulary of avant-garde design.[30] In that year Anthony Hunt was to write:

'Tweeds, and the simpler and firmer "folk weaves" form, to my mind, the most serviceable and appropriate material in which to clothe the architecturally conceived chairs and settees of to-day.'[31]

The Marcel Breuer and Alvar Aalto chairs of the mid 1930s amply illustrate Hunt's point (Fig 3.15). However, no Welsh mills were included to

Fig 3.15 Living room furniture by Marcel Breuer and F. R. S. Yorke for P. E. Gane Ltd. The white sycamore chairs are covered with Marianne Straub Welsh tweeds. 1935.

27 *Journal of the Rural Industries Bureau,* Winter 1936, p1.
28 Welsh tweeds sold through Gordon Russell Ltd were also exhibited by that firm, eg at the RIBA 'Design in Everyday Things' exhibition, 20 Feb–2 March 1936.
29 I am grateful to Maldwyn Williams, who by telephone and correspondence provided much information for this chapter.
30 Marianne Straub was replaced by Leonora Maas, who remained in Wales until the outbreak of war, whereupon she went to Gospels for approximately one year.
31 Hunt, Anthony, *Textile Design,* 'How to do it' series, The Studio Ltd, 1937, p68.

show in the 1935 Burlington House 'Exhibition of British Art in Industry', an oversight criticised at the time by Enid Marx because '. . . they are known to be doing some interesting experimental work' and represented 'one of the few real attempts to absorb art in industry in our own textile factories'.[32] Those who read the *Architectural Review*[33] would have been introduced to Welsh tweeds through an article which offered an alternative to the so severely criticised selection of products displayed at Burlington House. The illustrations for the AR article were collected by R. Dudley Ruder (organising secretary of the widely acclaimed 1933 Dorland Hall Exhibition) and showed woven furnishing fabrics by the Scottish Textile Weavers, Marion Dorn Ltd, Edinburgh Weavers, the Old Bleach Linen Co,

Donald Brothers, and Holywell Mill. All were tweeds showed the most natural similarity to the Bauhaus textiles. In 1939, at the suggestion of Herbert Read (author of the seminal work of the producing textured, striped or geometric designs, among which Marianne Straub's Holywell period on principles of design: *Art and Industry*), J.L. Martin and S. Speight published a book which outlined well designed furniture and equipment for the small home or flat.[34] Among the illustrations are a group of Holywell upholstery tweeds and a number of examples of their use by Gordon Russell Ltd, Marcel Breuer, P.E. Gane Ltd of Bristol, and Heal & Son Ltd (Fig 3.16). The latter two made note of the origins of the tweed in the caption, indicating the extent to which the Welsh woollens had become the 'dernier cri'.[35] (Fig 3.17)

THE ARCHITECTURAL REVIEW

Fig 3.16 Indian laurel furniture with chromium plate metal legs by E. Maxwell Fry and Jack Howe. Chairs covered in brown Welsh tweed, stocked by Heal & Son Ltd, 1935.

Fig 3.17 A Kensington living room, c1949, containing a 1946 Race DA4 settee covered with a Welsh tweed designed by Marianne Straub approximately ten years earlier. The large easy chair is by Heal's, the two-tiered table by Finmar and the coffee table by Ward & Austin (made up by the Scottish Furniture Manufacturers Ltd).

32   Marx, Enid, 'Textiles at the Exhibition of Industrial Art', *Design for Today,* vol III, March 35, 1935, p104.

33   *Architectural Review,* vol 78, p285.

34   Martin, J.L. and Speight, S., *The Flat Book,* William Heinemann, 1939.

35   Holywell Mill remains one of the 10–12 still in operation in Wales, employing the freelance designer, Beryl Gibson. Among their present range are cloths for high quality haute couture designers and retailers including Jaeger, who are thought to have used Holywell tweeds designed by Marianne Straub just prior to the Second World War, when they included Anny Blatt knitwear in their range. In 1984 Alan Schofield, Managing Director of Holywell Mill, invited Marianne Straub to re-work two of her mid '30s fashion fabrics for inclusion in the Holywell range.

Design for the retail trade: Helios

Helios, the company Marianne Straub joined as head designer in 1937, was formed in 1936 (Fig 4.1) as an independent subsidiary of Barlow & Jones Ltd, a century-old Lancashire firm which specialised in the manufacture of cotton goods and was one of Britain's best cotton spinners. Their wide range of cotton textiles was dominated by domestic items such as blankets, turkish towels, sheeting, bedspreads and quilts. The latter were a Barlow & Jones speciality, finely woven of Egyptian cotton with names, crests or monograms added at the request of the client. These, together with monogrammed sheets and towels, were supplied to leading hotels, steamship and railway companies and public institutions throughout the world. The waste yarn from these high-quality products was utilised for manufacture of cotton blankets, which an early 20th century report optimistically claimed were '. . . in enormous demand among the natives of Central and South Africa, by far the larger proportion of whom are clothed with Barlow and Jones' blankets.'[1] With dress linings, dress fabrics and mass-produced medium-priced furnishing fabrics also

in production, the inclusion of a range of exclusive, 'up-market' furnishing textiles was therefore a natural extension of Barlow & Jones' activities. The structure of Helios, with its relative independence from its parent company, was the idea of Barlow & Jones' Managing Director, Sir Thomas Barlow, and it clearly evolved from his commitment to raising standards in industrial design.

Barlow, born in 1883 into a prominent Manchester family, was by the age of 35 Managing Director of his family's textile firm and had already served five years on the board of Manchester's District Bank, of which he was to become Chairman in 1947. His position within Lancashire's business fraternity and his reputation as a man of great force and character led him to serve on numerous committees. At various times he was President of the Joint Committee of the Cotton Trades Organisation, Chairman of the Lancashire Industrial Development Council, as well as being Chairman of the Council of the Whitworth Art Gallery from 1930 to 1958. Most significant in the development of Helios, however, was his appointment to the Council for the Encouragement of Art in Industry in 1934 and his later chairmanship of its successor, the Council of Industrial Design, formed in 1944. This active participation in the development of British design awareness was combined with his lifelong love of the fine arts, out of which arose an excellent private collection. The Durers among them formed a group (now in the Melbourne Gallery, Australia) ranked in excellence with those held in the Albertina in Vienna and the British Museum in London. Barlow was therefore ideally qualified to bring art into conjunction with manufacturing. His wide ranging interest in the arts made him keenly aware of the developments taking place in the textile industry during the 1930s.

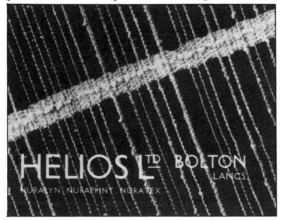

Fig 4.1 A Helios post-war publicity photograph, the background cloth of cotton, nuralyn, and wool.

By 1935, when Marianne Straub was working to raise design standards in Welsh woollens, several other textile manufacturers also had experimental units or studios producing advanced designs within their larger operations. Allan Walton Textiles, Foxton Ltd, Donald Brothers Ltd, Warner & Sons Ltd, Old Bleach Linen Company Ltd, and Morton Sundour's Edinburgh Weavers employed artists and designers of the highest calibre, producing contemporary textiles in keeping with modernist interiors. Barlow's desire to commit his firm to similar, high quality production was obviously well formed by 1935, when he happened to admire a particularly attractive tablecloth while visiting a friend. The owner of the cloth was Professor Loewe of Manchester University and the manufacturer was his brother-in-law, Felix Loewenstein, whose factory, 'Pausa', was near Stuttgart. Sir Thomas Barlow invited Mr Loewenstein to join the firm of Barlow & Jones and gave him the responsibility of setting up within the parent company a unit which was to bring to the furnishing fabric trade a range of high quality, aesthetically acceptable fabrics. Mr Loewenstein gave this newcomer the name of Helios.

Production at Helios began early in 1936, with the first designs by Frau Anny May, who had worked in the Pausa factory with Loewenstein. She came to Bolton for the initial few months and for a short period after her return to Germany both she and her husband continued to supply designs. The weaving was done in Barlow & Jones' Albert Mill no. 1, the Jacquards shared by both firms, with Stäubli dobbies brought in solely for Helios. As the firm of Helios was taking shape Marianne Straub was approached by the London representative for the Welsh Woollen mills, Miss Cadell, who was a distant relative of Sir Thomas. Miss Cadell suggested that Helios might provide an opportunity for interesting design work and a more settled lifestyle than that of a peripatetic designer for the Welsh mills. The final inducement was the discovery that the Helios dobbies were Stäublis (on Hattersly 4-box looms) with punched paper cards which were easy to make, light, and allowed for long repeats. Marianne Straub had used these looms in Switzerland and was impressed with their capabilities.

Sir Thomas was later to describe his ideal designer–manufacturer relationship, one which to all accounts very closely matched the working environment Marianne Straub was offered. He believed that:

'. . . design is essentially a team job. The designer, and this is equally applicable to the staff designer employed full time, must be given the information, the tools and the freedom of operation which will allow him to do his job properly. Manufacturers must see to it that the designer's path into a particular company is smoothed and that the technicians and engineers co-operate with him. The first step in such a process must, of course, be that of briefing the designer very thoroughly regarding the task he is expected to undertake. In fact, in choosing a designer, the manufacturer must, if he is to hope for successful result, state his needs very precisely.'[2]

Thus when Marianne Straub joined Helios on 2 March 1937, she was given the freedom and support as head designer to develop a range of woven and printed fabrics which largely reflected her own philosophy of design (Fig 4.2).

1   'The Complete Cotton Manufacturer: One of the oldest firms in the Cotton Industry', Supplement to *The Illustrated London News,* 10 July 1909, pXII.
2   Barlow, Sir Thomas D., 'Introduction', *Designers in Britain,* Allan Wingate vol 1, 1949, p190.

Whereas Marianne Straub's work at Gospels was entirely concerned with hand production and thus considered as a craft activity, her design task for the Welsh mills was concerned with mechanical spinning and powerloom weaving and hence was an industrial design activity. However, in both contexts the contact between designer and product was constantly maintained. Because the Welsh mills were small and the machinery geared to comparatively short production runs Marianne Straub had not yet had to face up to the implications of mass production in its 1930s context. The move to Bolton gave her this opportunity.

Yarns had to be bought in from various spinners, although Barlow & Jones — famous for their fine cotton yarns — did supply a small proportion from their own production (most notably Nuralyn, a combination of rami and cotton created by Loewenstein and confined to Helios except for use as a knitting yarn). All yarn dyeing was carried out by specialist firms to the highest possible standards of colour fastness and, since dye-batches were a minimum of 350 lbs per colour, the range had to be limited. 'A far cry from the happy dyeing days at Ethel Mairet's, where by the evening, an exciting collection of newly dyed hanks would hang in the weaving room.'[3]

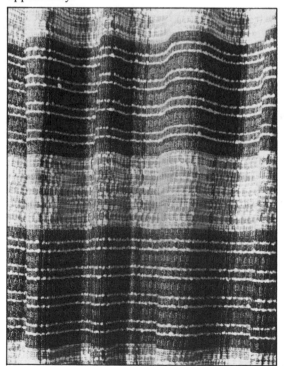

Fig 4.2 A dobby-woven curtain of cotton and fibro, the first designed by Marianne Straub for Helios.

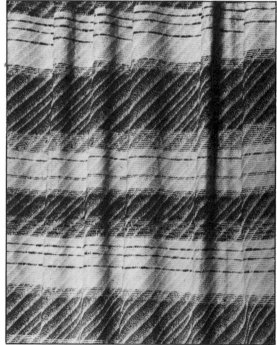

Fig 4.3 One of the first dobby-woven curtain fabrics produced at Helios to Marianne Straub's design. It was exhibited at the Red Rose Guild in 1937 or '38.

Prior to the war the Helios range consisted mainly of curtain material (Fig 4.3).[4] Worsted, linen and cotton yarns of a standard nature were combined with an ever increasing range of 'fancy' yarns — knop yarns, crimp yarns, slub yarns — and yarns spun from manmade fibres (viscose rayon being the most important of these fibres at that time). Texture became a most important adjunct to colour and tended to supersede formal design, which itself began moving away from rhythmic geometric motifs toward more flowing graceful lines in 1937. As the Stäubli dobbies had been specially installed for the use of Helios, the early range was designed specifically for these machines. In the two pre-war years only a few Jacquard designs were introduced into the range, together with a handful of upholstery cloths (Fig 4.4).

With the outbreak of war in 1939 the colours within one cloth were reduced to two or three.

Fig 4.5 Helios Jacquard blackout cloths 'Roseley', 'Monmouth' and 'Mirik' by Marianne Straub, 1940–41.

Fig 4.4 Furnishing fabrics, c1938/9 (left to right) 'Barra', 'Chelsea', and 'Stroma', the latter was the first Jacquard in Marianne Straub's Helios range.

3   Marianne Straub.
4   It is thought that all written records of the Helios production have been lost or destroyed. A number of samples remain, however, held in the Victoria & Albert Museum in London, the Warner Archive in Braintree, and the Whitworth Art Gallery and Gallery of English Costume in Manchester. The same collections hold examples of her work for Warners.

Sir Thomas Barlow, as Director General of Civilian Clothing, controlled the distribution of cotton yarns and, as is often the case, his 'child', Helios, was always last to receive its allocation. Production of some standard furnishing cloths continued, together with black-out cloths (Fig 4.5). These *had* to be absolutely opaque. To obtain the required specification, a coloured warp was very densely set, using Nuralyn, rayon or a slubby fibro yarn, the weave based on a satin sequence. The weft was of a condenser cotton quality, dyed black or, in exceptional cases, very dark shades. The latter was done to avoid the inevitable black which, although not necessary, characterised all these cloths.

Fig 4.6 Mock-leno cloth of linen with gold metal thread developed for tablecloth c1941 and selected six years later for inclusion in the first volume of the SIAD's Designers in Britain.

In between coping with the day-to-day business affairs of the firm during the war years, Marianne Straub experimented with new design ideas which could not be put into immediate production, but formed an invaluable reserve after the war when restrictions were gradually relaxed and production returned to normal (Fig 4.6). Throughout, she continued to produce approximately 50 new designs a year. Using what odd unrestricted yarns she could locate together with pre-war stocks, some special pieces were woven when the opportunity arose and 'allocated' to favourite clients who had been supportive before the war.

One of the most taxing jobs during the years of restrictions was choosing a colour palette which had then to remain in use for some years. While there was a wide range of yarns available up to 1940, yarn stocks became increasingly restricted as the war progressed, prohibiting speculative intake of both fancy-effect yarns and new colours. The norm at Helios was five or six standard yarns each dyed in up to ten or twelve colours. During the war a new colour range had to be devised by introducing colours in one yarn which could be combined with the colours in stock to give maximum flexibility. Differnt fibres demanded different colours and this too had to be taken into account. For example, Nuralyn had a brilliant, beautiful sheen, whereas cotton had considerably less reflective qualities. To use them together the Nuralyn had to be dyed in soft colours and the cotton in bright colours, thereby allowing their respective surface qualities to bring the colour-effect into the same tonal range. Standards of fastness to light further restricted colour choice, virtually eliminating bright yellow, pinks and some light blues from the Helios range (Fig 4.7). At the beginning of the War a fast blue/green was introduced, and Marianne Straub first saw it at one of the early Colour, Design and Style Centre exhibitions: 'One great boost from ICI!'[5]

Despite these restrictions, Helios became known for its skilful use of the new novelty yarns available to industry (Fig 4.8). Marianne Straub gained a reputation for being very critical in her selection of yarns, demanding both practicality and visual interest. Many were supplied by R. Greg & Co Ltd, whose sales director, Stopford Jacks, knew that, 'She had an acute sense of texture and colour; her standards were very high. Without doubt she and Alastair Morton were the most experienced, knowledgeable and practical weavers in the country.'[6] Alastair Morton was in residence at Gospels during the winter of 1943/44, when Marianne Straub was also there. 'Whilst Edinburgh Weavers lay dormant, Alas-

tair Morton concentrated on other creative pursuits including painting and photography, so coming to Gospels was his way of getting back into the textile design world.'[7] Their respective firms worked together on a number of occasions. When Helios had more weaving than it could accommodate, it was put out to Morton Sundour which also wove for Edinburgh Weavers, where

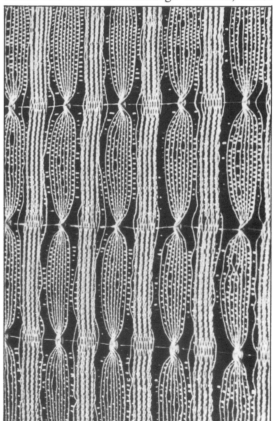

Fig 4.8 Experimental leno weave employing cellophane, 1939.

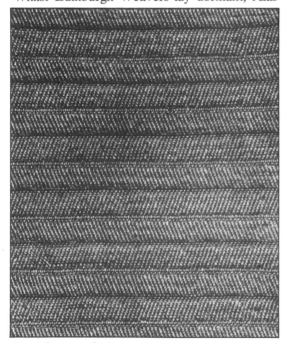

Fig 4.7 An upholstery cloth with a mohair face and cotton backing developed in 1942 in three colourways: greyish blue with a red warp stripe, nigger with yellow, and red with light blue.

5   Marianne Straub.
6   Correspondence from Stopford Jacks, 8 June 1983.
7   Marianne Straub.

'... there had been nothing doing since the outbreak of war.'[8] Much of the dyeing for Helios was done by Morton Sundour, pioneers of research into dyestuffs under the direction of Alastair's father, Sir James Morton. The Morton Sundour subsidiary, Edinburgh Weavers, was created 'to design and make fabrics for individual jobs, collaborating with the architect or decorator in each case',[9] although they did increase their production of stock for retailers in the 1950s. Helios, in contrast, produced a handful of fabrics for special projects, but largely aimed its production at the newly selective middle class market.[10] Its retail range was the first available to the general public which had been exclusively designed and supervised by a highly skilled designer.

The Helios range included a collection of hand screen-printed furnishing fabrics, commissioned

COURTESY OF WARNER & SONS LTD

Fig 4.9 'Sutherland Rose' designed by Graham Sutherland in 1940 and purchased by Marianne Straub for Helios from the Colour, Design and Style Centre.

or bought from a number of freelance designers by Marianne Straub and Felix Loewenstein. Helios purchased several of their print designs from the first Colour, Design and Style Centre exhibition in the winter of 1940–41. The exhibition was organised by Gerald Holtom, who was requested to do so as a result of a thesis he had written on printed textile design and sent to Sir Thomas Barlow.[11] He asked a number of artists to submit designs, including Eric Ravillious, Frances Lowe, Graham Sutherland, John Piper, Edward Bawden, John Aldridge, Duncan Grant and Vanessa Bell. Only a few of the designs purchased actually went into production and the most successful of these was Sutherland's 'Rose' (Fig 4.9). As a result of its inclusion in the 'Britain Can Make It' exhibition it became one of the most widely illustrated prints of the period and continued in production at Warners well into the 1950s.

Several designs were purchased in Germany, France (Studio Rosal, Paris), Belgium (Händel Design Studio, Brussels) and in Switzerland from the freelance designer Noldi Soland, who principally designed for French manufacturers. Only one, 'Wychwood', was produced and, like the Sutherland 'Rose', remained in the range from its introduction, in about 1938, into the early 1950s. Other print designs were purchased from Hans Tisdell, Jacqueline Groag, Jane Edgar, Marianne Mahler, Rex Whistler, Oliver Messell, Ronald Grierson and Margaret Meades (Fig 4.10). A number of designs were provided by Margaret Simeon, who was then teaching at St Martin's School of Art and was contacted by Loewenstein. Marianne Straub occasionally visited the Central School of Art in London, which was well known at the time for printed textile design. There she purchased designs from students. She also purchased designs from an ex-Central student, Sylvia Priestley, introduced to Helios through the Council of Industrial Design (Fig

4.11). Her designs typify the Helios printed textile range, with boldly drawn floral patterns employing flat stylised shapes accented with energetic line details.

For a short period when Marianne Straub was absent from Helios, Otti Berger was retained to design woven cloths. A handful of woven designs were purchased, including 'Stars and Stripes' from Jane Edgar, which remained in the Heal's range for over a decade, woven first at Helios and subsequently at Warners. Dora Batty, head of the textile department at the Central School, designed for Barlow & Jones and was commissioned by Helios for both printed and Jacquard-woven designs. Helios also developed a range of glass fabrics; both continuous filament glass yarn and spun glass fibre yarns were available unrationed. These cloths were woven in a plain weave construction and either piece dyed or printed

with pigment dyes. At least one printed fibreglass fabric was designed by the wood engraver, John Farleigh, and printed in gold pigment (Fig 4.12). It was exhibited among the 20 or so Helios fabrics in the 'Britain Can Make It' exhibition of

PHOTO JOHN GAY

Fig 4.11 Printed furnishing fabric by Sylvia Priestley, produced by Helios, c1948.

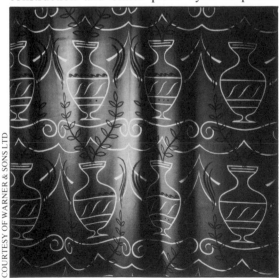

COURTESY OF WARNER & SONS LTD

Fig 4.10 'Dean' a printed cotton designed by Jane Edgar and printed by Helios c1946. Helios also purchased her designs for use in their wovens range.

8 Calvocoressi, Richard 'Introduction', *Alastair Morton and Edinburgh Weavers: Abstract Art and Textile Design 1933–46*, Scottish National Gallery of Modern Art, 1978, p7.

9 Morton, Jocelyn *Three Generations in a Family Textile Firm*, Routledge & Kegan Paul, 1971, p296.

10 In 1940 The Gallery of English Costume, Platt Hall, was given seven 3.5 yard lengths of Helios fabrics, each valued at £1 10s.

11 Interview of Gerald Holtom by Deborah Barker, 25 January 1983, p4.

1946. Contemporary observers were struck with the way in which the minimum of resources were used to achieve the maximum in effect.[12]

The war years are generally regarded as a contracted period of style development, yet the foundations laid during these years were significant to the production and consumption of

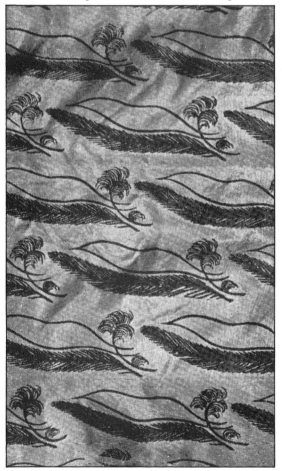

Fig 4.12 'Kew' by John Farleigh, a gold pigment print on fibreglass included in the 'Britain Can Make It' exhibition in 1946.

textiles for several decades afterwards (Fig 4.13). In 1940 the Cotton Board established the Colour, Design and Style Centre in Manchester, the heart of Britain's cotton industry. After an uneasy start, J. Cleveland Belle (director of the Centre until 1950) established a reputation for 'startling and original'[13] exhibitions, of which there were on average, five a year. The Centre concentrated on raising design standards of printed cotton fashion fabrics, and maintaining a register of textile designers. Its progressive exhibition policy included showing fabrics from foreign markets and accompanying well designed British textiles with furniture, pottery, glass and wallpaper. In the latter type of exhibition Helios fabrics were often included, and Marianne Straub maintained close contact with the Centre, being one of the few textiles designers 'on hand' in nearby Bolton.

The Centre was the creation of Sir Raymond Street, Chairman of the Cotton Board, who claimed that he thought of the idea in the bath and '. . . didn't pull out the plug, but let the idea grow.'[14] Many other ideas were growing in other design-conscious minds, including Sir Thomas Barlow's. He had been closely involved at the highest political level in the discussions in the early 1940s which led to the formation by Hugh Dalton (President of the Board of Trade) of the Council of Industrial Design (CoID) in 1944 and, as its first Chairman (until 1947), had considerable influence on its early course. The most notable event under his chairmanship was

12   I am indebted to Donald Tomlinson for this and other comments on the impact of Helios which he outlined in correspondence of 17 June 1983 and subsequently.

13   Farr, Michael *Design in British Industry,* 2nd edn, Cambridge University Press, 1955, p223.

14   Taped interview (no 1) with Marianne Straub, *op cit.*

15   Barlow, Sir Thomas D. 'The Council of Industrial Design', *Design 46: Survey of British Industrial Design as Displayed at the 'Britain Can Make It' Exhibition,* HMSO, 1946, p7.

the 'Britain Can Make It' exhibition of 1946. Writing in a catalogue of the exhibition, Sir Thomas welcomed whatever controversy or criticism the selections might create, believing the interest would stimulate better quality and design as manufacturers re-converted to normal production.

'The war, and the economic situation which confronts the United Kingdom as a result of it, have brought industrial design on to the short list of problems urgently requiring solution, and as happens in so many cases have crystallised thinking about ways and means of achieving the solution.'[15]

Fig 4.13 An exhibition of English textiles at the Whitworth gallery in the winter of 1941–42, showing part of the Helios range, including prints by (from left) Marianne Mahler ('Epping', stocked by Dunn's of Bromley) and Noldi Soland ('Wychwood'). The Jacquard-woven fabrics are (from centre to right) two lengths of a design by Mr May surrounding 'Roselay' by Marianne Straub, 'Akaroa' by Dora Batty, and 'Timor' by Marianne Straub.

Much had been written on the influence of the Board of Trade's Utility Furniture scheme and its subsequent impact on furniture design, although less has been recorded regarding the influence of Utility Textile design, undertaken by Enid Marx in 1943 (Fig 4.14). The choice of a textile designer was made by Gordon Russell:

'When, during the war, as Chairman of the Utility Furniture Design Panel, I realised that we were coming to the end of stock materials I felt it was essential to try to improve the standard. I went to see the Yarn Controller (Sir Thomas Barlow) to find out what might be made available and with what limitations. I then went to see Ethel Mairet and Enid Marx's name cropped up as a possible designer. She proved interested in a very restricted job.'[16]

Given her close association with Sir Thomas and Ethel Mairet, together with her previous work for Gordon Russell at Holywell, it is no surprise that Marianne Straub was also approached regarding the position. She turned it down, preferring to remain in Bolton and keep Helios alive for future, better days.

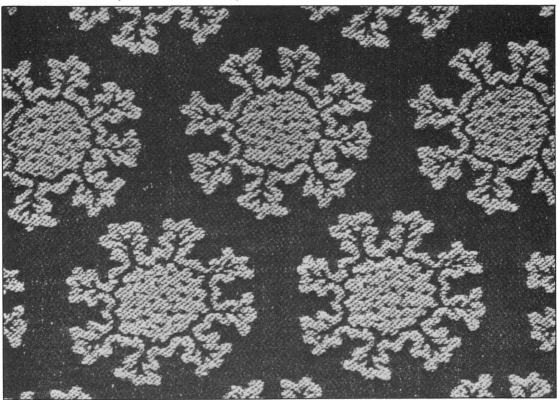

SIAD

Fig 4.14 Enid Marx utility furnishing cloth for the Board of Trade, 1943–45.

During her three years as utility fabric designer, Enid Marx did much to improve the quality of popular-priced fabrics, bringing well designed products to a market which had previously been ignored in favour of the exclusive client. It is within this context that the post-1940 Helios production must be considered. Donald Tomlinson, Director of the Colour, Design and Style Centre from 1950 to 1964, emphasises:

'. . . the extent to which popular priced fabrics were patterned, crammed with incident and decoration. It was to combat the vulgarity of many of these florals, folk weaves and ethnics for which the Utility Scheme had prepared the way that made the Helios experiment truly significant.'[17]

The stylistic achievements of Helios were three-fold. First, simple motifs predominated in a period which embraced pattern, described vividly by Donald Tomlinson as:

'. . . distortions of the Omega workshop fabrics pioneered by Heals; . . . central European 'folk weaves' and innumerable stripes loosely derived from alien archaic sources. One is left with the memory of a plethora of small-scale stripes of figures marching in opposing directions in alternating horizontal stripes; of a vast series of miniaturised friezes loosely derived from the far flung corners of the British Museum.'[18]

Secondly, the simple motifs were given maximum impact through the use of fancy yarns and subtle weaves (Figs 4.15 & 4.15a). Many fabrics employed a satin ground against a slubbed figure — often reduced to a single line outline. Two or more fancy yarns were often combined so as to appear to lie on the surface of the fabric, while actually securely anchored within the structure of the cloth. Finally, the colour palette, a chalky

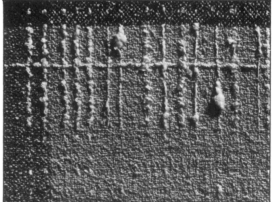

Fig 4.15 and 4.15a 'Perth' and 'Elgin' (detail), two of four cotton and fibro furnishing fabrics developed by Marianne Straub on the same warp, 1938.

16   Russell, Gordon, 'Designs for Industry' *Enid Marx*, Camden Arts Centre, 1979, p14.

17   Correspondence from Donald Tomlinson, *op cit* p3.

18   *Ibid.*

madder-red, blue and green was regarded as sophisticated yet fresh. In Marianne Straub's 'cross-word puzzle mind'[19] designing for Helios became a game of endless permutations based on limited factors.

Kathleen Fleetwood, assistant in the design studio from 1937 to 1949, ably summarises the method of design development at Helios:

'It was in the dobby-woven area that Helios set the most new and exciting approaches and standards. Miss Straub was not only an outstandingly creative person who also possessed a thorough understanding of textile technology — she was, in addition to this, a very skilled hand-craftsman. Our design prototypes were evolved by the extremely flexible methods of experimental work on handlooms — not a common practice in our industry in this country at that time. Miss Straub developed and modified her initial ideas according to the behaviour and appearance of the various yarns and structures as she wove them on the handloom. With her very advanced appreciation of the possibilities inherent in weaving for the exploitation of texture, both by contrasts of weave-structure and by the employment together of yarns of different natural origin, thickness and texture — together with her inventive use of the scope provided by carefully planned 'drafting' — Miss Straub created fabrics with fresh and exciting surface qualities, texture contrasts and colour combinations; fabrics which had small relationship to the more usual 'twill variant', 'shadow-stripe', 'all-over broken effect' and 'folkweave' industrial dobby fabrics of that period.'[20] (Figs 4.16 & 4.17)

The Helios range was marketed through the Barlow & Jones showroom in Maidstone House, Berner Street, London. Prior to the war there were three members of staff who, among other duties, occasionally acted as sales representatives. All joined the forces. Robert Isherwood went to the parent company's offices in Manchester on his return, and Norman Tomlinson rejoined Helios to assist with the running of the firm. Joyce Revell (née Fiske) joined Kathleen Fleetwood in the design studio as an apprentice for a short period after the war. The latter recollects over 40 firms which sold Helios fabrics, these well distributed across the UK and as far afield as South Africa and Reykjavik. In 1948 Helios appointed a full-time salesman, Douglas Kitching, who had been with Warner & Sons

Fig 4.16 Marianne Straub surrounded by Helios fabrics of 1947–49.

prior to the war. He extended the clients of Helios, and recalls that many shops were not as committed to modern design as, for example, Dunn's of Bromley, which by 1939 was 90 per cent modern. Thus many modern departments existed as the result of an enthusiastic buyer, George Breeze at Lewis's, Manchester and Victor Sawtell at Bowman's, Campden Town notable among them.[21]

Dunn's of Bromley and Heal's were early supporters of Helios, the Heal's records showing over 40 designs selected between 1938 and 1940 (Fig 4.18). Other retailers who offered Helios fabrics to their customers were Gane's of Bristol,

Fig 4.17 'Solway', an all-cotton wartime Helios furnishing cloth by Marianne Straub.

Rowntree's of Scarborough, Mummery and Harris of Frinton, Grant's of Glasgow, Bentalls in Kingston-upon-Thames, Storey's and Maples in London, Lewis's and Bowman's. Many of these joined the Good Furnishing Group in 1938, an association of retailers formed by Geoffrey Dunn, Gordon Russell and Crofton Gane to collectively commission designs which, once produced, would be stocked simultaneously. Before the war supressed the Group, the scheme produced an easy chair by Howard Keith and a dining room suite by Gordon Russell Ltd, both of which were shown at the British Industries Fair (BIF) in 1939.[22] Both firms used Helios fabrics (Fig 4.19), as did two further exclusive London shops: Ian Henderson & Co and Dunbar-Hay. Ian Henderson was an interior decorator and furniture designer, much of whose work was sold through Fortnum & Mason. At Dunbar-Hay, Cecilia Dunbar, now Lady Semple, commissioned 80 per cent of the stock. Many designs were supplied by students of the Royal College of Art, where Athole Hay was registrar. Most notable among their products were Eric Ravilious's urns and mugs manufactured by Wedgwood.

Up to and during the war Marianne Straub occasionally acted as 'rep' for Helios. In 1938, on her second trip to Finland, she took Helios samples to Alvar Aalto's shop, whose manager, Mr Halt, she had met two years before. He selected a few Jacquard designs, unusual in their use of birds. Geoffrey Dunn recalls a number of her visits and among her fabrics most particu-

19   Taped interview (no 2) with Marianne Straub, 24 May 1983.
20   Correspondence from Kathleen Fleetwood, 12 October 1983, pp4–5.
21   Interview with Douglas Kitching, 25 August 1983.
22   The Gordon Russell suite employs a tweed on the chair seat that is possibly one of Marianne Straub's Welsh tweed designs.

larly, the seersucker tablecloths (Fig 4.20), woven in checks, open 'plaids' or subtle stripes in chemically dyed colours which, in their shades and combinations, showed the designer's knowledge and love of natural dyes. In the furnishing cloths Dunn also remembers their good colouring and their neat, controlled designs which read well in any direction, making them ideally suited to Dunn's market. What Dunn appreciated in Marianne Straub's visits was that '. . . this was the *weaver,* the *designer,* coming to the shop!'[23] When later, in his lectures to the CoID, Dunn was to stress the importance of carpet and cloth designers keeping in touch with retailers and

Fig 4.18 A page from the Heal's guard book for 1940, showing Helios prints 'Epping', 'Wychwood' and 'Charnwood' in two colourways each and 'Sherwood' in one colourway. All were printed in a fibro/cotton/linen cloth and were stocked (price 9/11) in at least one colour until 1943. The top left fabric is by Foxtons.

their needs, one example he had in mind was Marianne Straub.

Most of the handful of commissions which Helios undertook came through contact with architects, including the fabrics for the New Cavendish Laboratories at Cambridge University. The interiors were designed by Lady Joan Worthington, who trained as an architect and worked in conjunction with her husband, Sir Bernard Worthington. Helios provided the bedspreads for the Savoy Hotel when it was redecorated by Peggy Rudd, who also supervised the refurbishment of Claridges and the Berkeley after the war. Marianne Straub designed a few

HK/PHOTO JOHN GAY

Fig 4.19 HK's 'Cavalier' settee, c1956, covered with a fabric designed by Marianne Straub and later produced by Warners.

23   Interview with Geoffrey Dunn, 30 September 1983.

bedspreads to introduce into the Helios range, but this was never undertaken. 'Pony' designed in 1940, was used by Lord Beaverbrook in his government office, and for the curtains in the first Council room of the CoID in Petty France in 1944 (Fig 4.21). Helios also provided all the fabrics for the new Balls Park, Bedfordshire teacher training college, and a number for the 'Empress of Canada.'

In 1947 Helios was commissioned to provide the fabrics for Cunard's 'Caronia', to be launched in 1948. The 'Caronia' interiors were supervised by Mr Leach, Cunard's interior architect. After discussing Helios samples with Marianne Straub, he arranged for her to visit Southampton, where the 'Queen Mary', the 'Caronia' and the 'Queen Elizabeth' were in dock. The 'Queen Elizabeth' was about to sail for New York, already having been refitted after war service. Marianne Straub was invited on to the 'Queen Elizabeth' to see the interiors and recalls enjoying her first unrationed luncheon since the beginning of the war.

The seating in the 'Caronia' public rooms was predominantly wood, leather and cane and the curtain fabrics designed to complement these relied on texture and movement for impact (Figs 4.22 & 4.23). The 'Norwich Stripe' employed weft fringing and was used over large areas in a number of the less formal public rooms. Its effect was striking, the severity of the broad horizontal bands broken by the gentle irregularity of the vertical rows of fringing within. In the bedrooms, matching curtains, pillowcases, and bedspreads were Jacquard woven in rayon and cotton (Figs 4.24 & 4.25). Several different designs were

HOUSE BEAUTIFUL

Fig 4.20 Marianne Straub's dining room at Great Bardfield, the table covered with a Helios cloth, St Mary (c1944), a dobby-woven 100% cotton for tablecloths and curtains, produced by Warners until c1957.

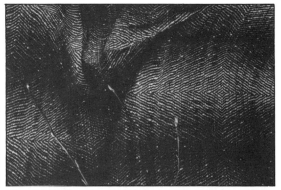

Fig 4.21 'Pony', employing a two-ply worsted weft and fancy cotton warp and used for curtains in the office of Lord Beaverbrook (1940) and those of the CoID in Petty France (1944).

used, all rare examples of Marianne Straub's fluency as a designer of large-scale abstract floral and geometric patterns. The 'Caronia' fabrics were well received and, as a result, Helios also contributed to the refurnishing of the 'Queen Mary' in 1949 (Figs 4.26 & 4.27).

Throughout her years with Helios, Marianne Straub lived in lodgings in Bolton, although from the outset she was a frequent weekend visitor at 'Firwood', where Margaret Pilkington lived with her parents and sister. In 1941 she spent four months there recuperating from a broken leg and by then had been adopted as a member of the family. Shortly afterwards both of Margaret Pilkington's parents died and Marianne Straub became a resident at 'Firwood', retaining her

PHOTO STEWART BALE

Fig 4.22 The 'Caronia' lounge/bar curtained in 'Norwich Stripe', 1947.

Fig 4.23 A 'Caronia' dining room with Helios Jacquard-woven curtains, designed by Marianne Straub.

Figs 4.24 & 4.25 Two of the alternative 'Caronia' bedroom schemes employing rayon and cotton Jacquard-woven cloths designed by Marianne Straub.

room in Bolton during the week (Fig 4.28).

Life at 'Firwood' was '... utterly unusual in the high degree of its cultivation' compared with the general atmosphere of Alderley Edge, in which it was located. The Edge in the first half of the century was 'not only not intellectual — it was very very English indeed — in its fear of the clever man and its fury at the clever woman.'[24]

Figs 4.26 & 4.27 Two of the refurbished 'Queen Mary' bedrooms, showing rayon and cotton Jacquard-woven soft furnishings similar to those designed by Marianne Straub for 'Caronia'.

By way of rebellion, the Pilkington sisters became 'clever women', Margaret Pilkington attending the Slade School prior to the First World War to study wood engraving. Aside from her creation of the Red Rose Guild as an outlet for professional craftsmen and her active support of the Whitworth Art Gallery, she maintained a wide-ranging interest in the cultural affairs of the area. As a result, 'Firwood' entertained guests from the world of the arts, crafts, music and literature (Fig 4.29). Elizabeth Wray, fashion writer and textile trade journalist, later editor of *Textiles International,* visited 'Firwood' on a number of occasions in the 1940s and '50s,

Fig 4.28 Firwood, Alderley Edge.

always looking forward to her trips to Manchester, when she would go out to the 'lovely, peaceful' Pilkington house, where the cultural life continued despite the war:

'... and one casually plucked a ripe peach from the wall as one wandered round the grounds or carefully cut a bunch of grapes from the hot house for the dining room table. This was a lovely house ... library and sofa table were casually, but liberally scattered with the sorts of books and art magazines that ... tempted one.'[25]

Margaret Pilkington (Fig 4.30) and Marianne Straub had many friends and interests in com-

Fig 4.29 The room at Firwood which Marianne Straub used as her study, containing furniture with loose linen covers, Jacquard-woven by Old Bleach Linen Company.

24   Unpublished manuscript of a lecture on Margaret Pilkington by Sir William Mansfield Cooper on the occasion of the Friends of the Whitworth Art Gallery's 50th Anniversary, 5 May 1983, pp9–10.

25   Correspondence from Elizabeth Wray, 20 June 1983.

mon, including their love of music. Until Margaret Pilkington's death in 1974 they remained great friends:

'The friendship extended to me by Margaret Pilkington and her sister Dorothy was most precious to me. To be adopted into the Pilkington family was a very great privilege. It gave me the opportunity to learn to appreciate the quality of the life of a highly cultured, socially conscious Manchester family. Sharing the life at Firwood with the Pilkington sisters was a wonderful experi-

Fig 4.30 Margaret Pilkington, early 1970s.

CHESHIRE LIFE

ence, for their interests were wide, and their willingness to share their friends unlimited. It was an opportunity to meet many interesting people who over the years have contributed to the richness of my life.'[26]

In 1947 Felix Loewenstein died and Marianne Straub became Managing Director of Helios, while still responsible for its artistic direction and the design of its wovens range. This was a task she found not to her liking, for it took her away from the full-time role as industrial designer that she had enjoyed for ten years. In consultation with Sir Thomas Barlow they decided in 1949 to sell Helios intact, although several other alternatives were considered.[27] Production at Helios continued apace, but it was a time of great despair, finally alleviated when Alec Hunter came forward with the suggestion of Warner & Sons Ltd that they take over Helios.

Marianne Straub and Alec Hunter had met at the end of the War, when Hunter came to Manchester for an SIA meeting. Margaret Pilkington had suggested that he be invited to stay at 'Firwood' and thus began a habit which continued until 1950: whenever Hunter came north he stayed at 'Firwood'. Both designers had much to discuss when they met at SIA meetings in London, and Marianne Straub made occasional visits to Hunter's family home in Thaxted. It was on her first visit to East Anglia, when the Hunters took her to Cambridge, that she decided it was an area she would like to live in, if ever a move from Bolton became necessary. She was thus delighted with the prospect of going to Warners, based in Braintree; more so because she knew of their reputation for high quality production and looked forward to working with yarns which were dyed at the mill.

Although in existence for only 14 years, Helios had made an impact which was not quickly forgotten. From 1937 their work had been exhibited and included in periodicals of books on good design. In 1951 the third volume of *Designers in Britain* — which, in 1947 and 1949, had included Marianne Straub's design among its exemplary wovens — illustrated two Helios wovens and two prints despite the fact that the firm no longer existed (Fig 4.31). In 1953 Michael Farr, in his follow-on from Pevsner's *Industrial Art in England,* concluded that a few firms, rather than the design centres[28] were responsible for establishing high design standards in furnishing textiles. He congratulated the handful of 'enlightened manufacturers' who not only proved that good design was commercially

Fig 4.32 *Designed by Marianne Straub in 1945, 'Monyash' (a rayon and cotton tissue) was chosen to illustrate Farr's* Design in British Industry *in 1953. He captioned the picture: 'To make good use of the different yarns within the capabilities of the Jacquard loom, the designer must work out the structure of the fabric himself. Here is a good example of the method naturally used to achieve an abstract pattern.'*

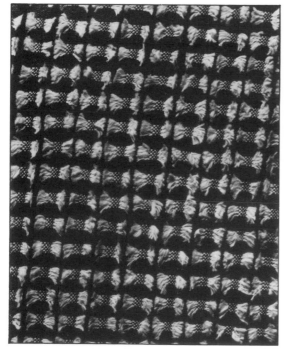

Fig 4.31 *'Thetford', c1947, a tufted cotton fabric, one of four Helios fabrics illustrated in* Designers in Britain *in 1951, a year after the company ceased production.*

26   Correspondence from Marianne Straub, 23 November 1983.
27   Joining Tibor Reich in running the newly-formed weaving firm backed by R. Greg & Co (yarn spinners) and returning to run Gospels were both considered.
28   He was referring to the Colour, Design & Style Centre, and the short-lived Rayon Industry Design and Interior Decoration Design Centres.

viable, but who were '... determined that their products should be of the highest artistic standard [which] is a matter of vital importance in any industry.'[29] Farr singled out three textile firms, one of which was Helios:

'Within two years the Helios range of inexpensive fabrics of exemplary design was attracting attention at all levels of the retail trade. A wide public was aimed at — a public, incidentally, which had never seen such designs outside the most exclusive shops. The credit for this achievement belongs to Marianne Straub, who has since been working on the same lines for Warner & Sons.'[30]

Of the nine illustrations chosen to illustrate good design, four are by Marianne Straub for Helios (two of which were later produced at Warners) (Figs 4.32 & 4.33). In the captions Farr stressed those qualities for which Marianne Straub is well known: her understanding of the looms, her sensitivity to yarns, and her 'organic' design method, whereby the structural and aesthetic components are developed simultaneously.

29 Farr, *op cit* p85.
30 *Ibid* p86.

Fig 4.33 'Prestbury' a dobby-woven fabric first produced by Helios in 1939 and later by Warners. Like the previous illustration, used by Farr and captioned: 'New fabrics should not be devised in vacuo, *but executed by the designer on an experimental loom. The industry in general does not believe this, and so fabrics like this where the subtlety of contrasting textures is vital, are rare.'*

Design for the contract trade
Warners

When Marianne Straub joined Warners on 1 May 1950, the firm was largely known for:

'... their immense range of skills, their ability to produce superbly crafted fabrics, frequently undertaking commissions for prestige projects of national significance where the sponsors' design briefs were clearly defined. It was their quality as producers rather than as design innovators that gave them unique status at that time.'[1]

This was an image which Warners acquired largely through their own choice, for although they had, since their foundation in 1870, produced both traditional and modern designs, *quality* and *tradition* were highly prized in the years immediately after the war. Further, the majority of Warner's modern designs throughout the 1930s and '40s were 'bespoke' (Figs 5.1 & 5.1a). Their fabrics for Hayes-Marshall of Fortnum & Mason, Dunn's of Bromley, Gordon Russell Ltd, Heal's, H.K. Furniture and others were identified in both contemporary and historical publications under the name of the retailer, leaving their contribution to contemporary design largely unknown to this day. To the casual observer, Warners' purchase of Helios and its range may have seemed out of character, but in fact this was not so, as a brief outline of the activities of several key figures at Warners shows.

Fig 5.1 An HK chair, c1937, covered with Fortnum and Mason's lining fabric printed by Warners at their Dartford printing works.

ARCHITECT'S JOURNAL/GORDON RUSSELL LTD

Fig 5.1a The London showroom of Gordon Russell Ltd, 40 Wigmore Street, c1936. The chair covering is 'Mendip' by Alec Hunter for Warners; the curtains are by Marianne Straub for Holywell Mill.

1   Correspondence from Donald Tomlinson. *op cit* p2.

Throughout his career, Sir Frank Warner, director of the firm from 1908 to 1930, was closely involved with both government and private organisations working towards the promotion of better design.[2] He was committed to improvement in the education of industrial designers: lecturing, examining, and sitting on Government committees to further these aims. Under his guidance the Royal Society of Arts initiated a national competition for design students in 1924, which continued for ten years, when they were re-organised into the present bursary awards. In addition he campaigned for the education of the general public and, as early as 1910, proposed a government council composed of artists, designers, industrialists and educationalists to oversee art and technical school training. Through an 'art-loving and art-seeking people' he believed, '... our manufacturers would be encouraged, indeed compelled, to meet the public demand for articles possessing artistic merit.'[3] In 1914 Harold Stabler and Ernest Jackson formed a 'committee of seven' which, in 1915, became the Design and Industries Association (DIA). Warner was one of the 11 signatories of their first memorandum and sat on the Council of the DIA until 1918. Having been an advisor to the Board of Trade during the First World War and a member of the Committee of the Board of Education in 1910–11 to report on the future of the Royal College of Art, Warner was instrumental in the formation of the British Institute of Industrial Art (BIIA), jointly mooted by both Boards. In 1918 he put forward the proposed aims of the BIIA at the Royal Society of Arts:

'The Institute would also provide the means of educating public taste and of guiding it on the right lines. ... It will possess and exercise a most important function in bringing designers and art workers into closer touch with original ideas and artistic taste; the industrial artist needs the opportunity of putting his activities to practical and profitable use. If the Institute can bring the two together it will in this respect alone more than have justified its existence.'[4]

The progress made by both organisations was slow: the BIIA did not survive to the end of the 1920s and by the early years of the 1930s the DIA '... was in danger of being left behind, with other bodies making use of its pioneer work and going beyond it.'[5] However individuals such as Sir Frank Warner did what they could. Power weaving was introduced at Warners in 1919 and art school-trained designers were employed. Designs were also purchased from students at colleges and through exhibitions. Further, Warner very closely matched the DIA ideal of the '... business man in his pleasant office, seeing to the proper housing of his workpeople in dignified factories, pleasantly equipped canteens and recreation rooms'[6] as records of Warner's 'New Mills' in Braintree show.

Sir Frank Warner was regarded by Pevsner as one of the initiators of the modern movement in English textiles, having '... consciously transferred the strong and indigenous tradition of exquisite (Spitalfields) weaving to the factory and carefully developed it there.'[7] Sir Frank never gave up his defence of designs based on traditional motifs, and at his death in 1930 left a legacy of forward-looking ideas on social and educational reform combined with concern for sound craftsmanship and lasting qualities in the firm's textile designs. His place as Managing Director was taken by Ernest Goodale (later Sir Ernest), his son-in-law. Goodale began an active campaign to widen the firm's range and to promote the fact that the firm did not only weave silk damasks in traditional designs. To further these aims he engaged Alec Hunter in 1932, the same year in which Marianne Straub began her studies at Bradford Technical College.

Hunter had spent the previous four years setting up the Edinburgh Weavers for James Morton (Fig 5.2). The cloths he designed were woven for Morton Sundour in Letchworth by his father's firm, St Edmundsbury Weavers. In late 1931 financial considerations forced Morton to move Hunter's experimental unit from Edinburgh to Carlisle, where the Morton firm's main

BRITISH ARCHITECTURAL LIBRARY/RIBA

Fig 5.2 A room designed by Maurice Adams in 1935, the sofa using 'Dunoon' designed by Alec Hunter for Edinburgh Weavers four years earlier.

2 For a full account of the work of Sir Frank Warner see Bury, Hester, *A Choice of Design*, Warner & Sons Ltd, 1981 and *Weaving and the Warners* (see note 10 below).

3 Lecture by Sir Frank Warner to Bradford School of Art, 11 January 1911, p7; unpublished typescript, Warner Archive.

4 Warner, Sir Frank, 'Report of a lecture to the Royal Society of Arts' *Journal of the Royal Society of Arts,* 1 November 1918, p23.

5 *Year Book 1964–5* Design and Industries Assoc, p234.

6 MacCarthy, *op cit* p80.

7 Pevsner, 'An Inquiry . . .', *op cit* p55.

operation was located, but where Hunter and his wife were not prepared to go. In 1932 Edinburgh Weavers was put under the charge of Morton's son, Alastair, whose considerable achievements thereafter in modern textile design are well known.[8] Hunter, however, had already established a successful base for future developments. Fabrics were stocked by Heals, Gordon Russell Ltd, and Libertys and generated considerable comment both in America and in Europe when they were exhibited at the Monza International Exhibition in 1930. In 1931 they received the contract for furnishing Broadcasting House, a prestigious project for which the architects (J. Val Myers and F.J. Watson-Hart) initially proposed modern German fabrics. Roger Smithells, writing in *Decoration* in 1937, marked the eventual outcome as a turning point:

> 'Fortunately there were then some British manufacturers, notably the Edinburgh Weavers, sufficiently alive to the situation to step into the breach. They undertook to make the fabrics required and the production of contemporary British fabrics had at last begun.'[9]

A number of Hunter's designs, including several for Broadcasting House, proved so popular that they continued to be produced by Edinburgh Weavers throughout the 1930s.

Hunter had been brought up in his father's weaving firm, the St Edmundsbury Silk Weavers, and therefore had considerable experience with both woven techniques and the running of the business. Goodale was certain he had chosen the right man to whom to entrust Warner's contemporary range:

> 'Hunter combined a rare appreciation of the beauties of the past ... with a desire to create for and of the present. ... He also had an unusual regard for costs and costing.'[10]

With Hunter's guidance, Warner's were able to increase their range *and* make a profit, something which was not typical in firms producing a modern 'up-market' range.[11] This was achieved by introducing the use of linen, cotton and rayon into the power-woven cloths and, of course, by producing successful designs. They were thus able, in 1934, to sell their power-wovens at eight to sixteen shillings a yard, compared with 30 shillings a yard for hand-woven damasks and up to £5 a yard for exclusive fabrics. Although the power-wovens sold in the upper end of the price range for mass-produced furnishing fabrics (recalling that Marianne Straub's Welsh tweeds at Gordon Russell Ltd sold for 8–9 shillings a yard in 1936), they represented an effort to answer criticisms voiced over the exclusivity of many objects shown in exhibitions promoting good modern design. The range at this time contained over 1500 designs — 50–80 new designs being introduced each year — and this was in addition to those produced to special order.

To produce such a wide range a number of freelance designers were employed. Through Hunter's active participation in the SIA a number of established designers were sought out, including Louise Aldred, Eva and Hans Aufseeser (Tisdall), Margaret Simeon, Eva Crofts and Marion Dorn. All designed hand screen-printed fabrics, produced in the firm's Dartford printworks from 1932. Warners were among the first commercial hand screen-printers in the UK and undertook commission printing for Eileen Hunter and Footprints. Marion Dorn also supplied woven designs (Fig 5.3), which were developed in conjunction with Alec Hunter, who encouraged her experimental use of effect yarns such as Astrakan and Viscut, and techniques such as fringing and tufting. Her prints and wovens were sold either through Warners or her own shop, Marion Dorn Ltd. which opened in 1934.

Of greater importance to Marianne Straub, however, was the fact that Hunter himself was keen to introduce new fibres and weaves. After his appointment in 1932, Warner's woven cloths showed a more adventurous use of rayon, linen, cotton and wool, often in combination with Warner's traditional fibre, silk. Like Marianne Straub, Hunter designed his cloths on the hand loom, resulting in the introduction of warp-faced tapestry and supplementary weft weaves to the powerloom production (Fig 5.4). The tapestry technique, whereby the design was created by the vertical threads alone, resulted in a very thick fabric particularly suitable for public interiors. It was used by Hunter for some of Warners most prestigious commissions during the 1930s: for the RIBA headquarters, opened in 1934 (Fig 5.4a); the RMS 'Queen Mary', launched in 1936,[12] and for the University of London Senate House, designed by Charles Holden in 1938.

Hunter was actively involved in running the factory and formulating the firm's design policy, becoming a director in 1943. He encouraged the establishment of a craft-weaver's studio within

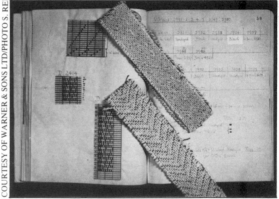

COURTESY OF WARNER & SONS LTD/PHOTO S. REDMAN

Fig 5.4 One of Marianne Straub's technical books from the 1970s (shown together with the handwoven prototypes) with weave details for two variations on the same warp.

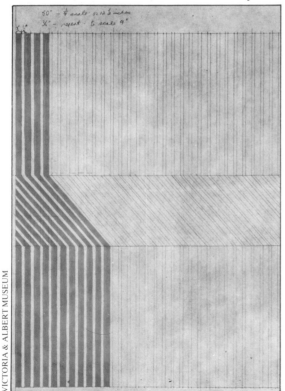

VICTORIA & ALBERT MUSEUM

Fig 5.3 Design by Marion Dorn for a woven fabric, c1935, produced by Warners.

8 See Morton, *op cit,* Farr, *op cit,* and Pevsner, *op cit.*

9 Smithells, Roger 'Fabrics of 1937' *Decoration,* 1937, p45.

10 Goodale, Sir Ernest *Weaving and The Warners* F. Lewis Publishers Ltd, 1971, p40.

11 For example, Edinburgh Weavers was supported by the 'bread and butter' lines of Morton Sundour and Helios only made very small profits. The *Observer,* 22 September 1946, records that '. . . like most such attempts, Helios incurred substantial losses at the start', although Marianne Straub disputes the extent to which this is true.

12 Warners produced the majority of the fabrics for the Queen Mary, both printed and woven.

the mill, which became financially possible in 1935 and was set up by Theo Moorman. With all facilities and materials provided, Theo Moorman was free to experiment, employing the firm's name and thus having a ready market for her work. She designed both for small, specialised orders and for production at the mill. Although her work was cut short by the outbreak of war in 1939, she produced a notable group of fabrics employing gimp, snarl, and other looped and textured yarns, often with simple, striking inlaid designs (Fig 5.5). The results of her '. . . laboratory work of the greatest potential value'[13] were largely cushion covers, which sold for approximately 16/6d at design-conscious retailers such as Dunn's of Bromley. Lengths were also produced, these selling at retail outlets including Gordon Russell Ltd and Heals. These firms' records show that Warners not only supplied fabrics from their experimental unit, but also from among those designed by both freelance and in-house designers, including Hunter, Albert Swindells, Herbert Woodman and Bertrand Whittaker. Thus, in the second half of the 1930s, Warners' modern production represented a well integrated selection of designs from a wide

Fig 5.4a The first floor gallery of the Royal Institute of British Architects' building, 1934, the windows hung with 'Crosby' by Alec Hunter for Warner & Sons Ltd.

Fig 5.5 The Warner London showroom as redesigned by Wells Coates, showing a group of Theo Moorman weaves as they were displayed when the showroom was opened by Frank Pick, on 9 November 1936.

BRITISH ARCHITECTURAL LIBRARY/RIBA

COURTESY OF WARNER & SONS LTD

variety of sources, many of which were sold exclusively through other wholesalers, as were Marianne Straub's designs later on.

Reproductions and designs based on traditional sources remained an important part of the range for, like Sir Frank Warner, Hunter maintained a healthy respect for the past, a characteristic which may well distinguish English 'modernists' from continental. Allen Walton, director of Allen Walton Ltd and manufacturer of a fine range of modern hand screen-prints from 1933 to 1948, expressed a view typical of many, when in 1935 he stated that the artist craftsman '. . . is there to sift the experience of the past and to draw on his imagination for the future.'[14] Goodale, too, enthusiastically supported Hunter in his belief that:

'The best modern design is not divorced from the past, and a firm with a great tradition should be among those who lead in such work, for where there is no tradition design becomes sterile. To live entirely in the past is to die, but to be proud of one's tradition and to live in the present is, I think, to live well.'[15]

Goodale, a solicitor not 'brought up' to the textile trade, nevertheless quickly took up another Warner tradition — that of active involvement in textile trade and Government organisations. Other members of the Warner and Sons Ltd Board had similar interests. A past Chairman and Vice President of the Council of the RSA was John A. Milne, Managing Director of Henry Stone & Son Ltd, furniture manufacturers, and a leading exponent of the cause of good design in industrial products. His friendship with Sir Frank Warner led to his invitation to join the board of Warners in 1930, where he served until 1955. Goodale became a member of the CoID at its formation in 1944, remaining until 1949 when he became Chairman of the RSA.

The majority of his years with the CoID were under the chairmanship of Sir Thomas Barlow. Quite naturally, when the future of Helios and Marianne Straub were under consideration, Barlow entered into discussion with Goodale, certain both of Warner's commitment to modern textile production and the larger issues of the day. To Goodale, the opportunity to take over a very interesting range of modern woven fabrics was in line with his own thinking, and he had Alec Hunter's enthusiastic support in doing so.[16]

The respective associations between managing directors and head designers of Helios and Warners aside, one further factor indicated the logic of amalgamating one into the other: the retail outlets which they commonly supplied. This was partly due to the small number which actively sought out and supported modern design in the years immediately before and after the war, resulting in an 'extended family' of manufacturers, designers, retailers and salesmen. That the terms 'pioneer', 'crusader' and 'missionary' frequently aligned themselves to members of this group is not without significance, and neither is it surprising that close contact existed among all.

For example, Hayes-Marshall, who early in the 1930s 'started buying and got everyone

13   Smithells, *op cit.* Pevsner, in 'Design Parade', *The Studio*, vol 119, January–June, 1940, p183, notes that the workshop was set up 'because Miss Moorman and Warners and a few progressive buyers felt that it should be possible to do something in this country to take the place of exquisite woven materials imported from certain workshops in Denmark, Holland and Germany. Miss Moorman's work has shown that this aim can be reached.'

14   Walton, Allen 'The Artist and the Machine', lecture read to the RSA and reported in the *Journal of the Royal Society of Arts*, February 1935, p69. I am indebted to Deborah Barker, who drew my attention to this article.

15   Goodale, Sir Ernest 'A History of Warner & Sons Ltd', *Journal of the Textile Institute*, February 1950, p46.

16   Interview with Sir Ernest Goodale, 16 October 1983.

buying'[17] commissioned fabrics from Warners exclusively for Fortnum & Mason, many of which were sent to H.K. Furniture to be made up to Hayes-Marshall's requirements. At the same time, H.K. also bought cloth directly from Warners. Founded by Howard Keith in 1933, H.K. became market leaders in the 1950s, during which time they made extensive use of the upholstery cloths produced in Wales, designed by Marianne Straub. They also used Helios fabrics and, in the 1950s, her fabrics produced at Warners. One of the first retailers to stock H.K. furniture was Dunn's of Bromley, at the instigation of Geoffrey Dunn. Dunn had begun introducing modern stock into his family's store in 1932 and, by 1938, was selling textiles by Helios,

Warners (Fig 5.6), Edinburgh Weavers, Donald Brothers, and Ernest Race, the latter better known for cast aluminium and steel rod furniture. Geoffrey Dunn, as a member of the selection committee for the CoID's 'Britain Can Make It' exhibition in 1946, saw the prototypes of Race's 'BA' chair and placed the first order to the newly formed Ernest Race Ltd. Another member of the same selection committee, Anthony Heal, placed the second order.[18] The chairs were covered with Welsh tweeds designed

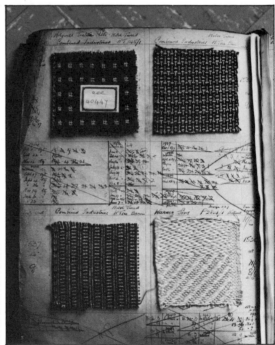

Fig 5.7 A page from a Heal's guard book, recording fabrics in stock in 1934. The bottom right cloth was designed by Alec Hunter and made by Warners exclusively for Heal's. The remainder are Welsh tweeds, two by Marianne Straub, the third (top left) by Gerd Bergerson. All but one cloth remained in stock until 1941.

COURTESY OF GEOFFREY DUNN

Fig 5.6 A leaf from a 1938 Dunn's of Bromley catalogue including four Warners fabrics: 'Mollusc' (no 5) and 'Lilium' (no 2) by Herbert Woodman, 'Clematis' (no 4) by Louise Aldred, and no 13, probably by Theo Moorman.

some ten years earlier by Marianne Straub. At Heal's, a glance at the order books from the textile department tell a similar story (Fig 5.7). In 1939, for example, among stock ordered from Allan Walton, Donald Brothers, Sandersons, Turnbull and Stockdale, and Edinburgh Weavers, are Helios wovens and prints, Warners wovens and prints (including one by Paul Nash reserved to Heal's) and Holywell woollens, designed by Marianne Straub five years earlier. Heal's were later to have remarkable success with Marianne Straub's fabrics for Warners (see p 000).

As buyers, Dunn and Heal had considerable influence on the public's perception of 'good taste' throughout the middle years of the century, together with Pevsner and Dick Russell at Gordon Russell Ltd's Wigmore Street showroom. It has already been noted that Gordon Russell Ltd had taken Welsh woollens into their stock in 1935, and these cloths were still used on some furniture manufactured in Broadway well after the war. In 1935 Wigmore Street also showed samples of Warners' prints and wovens and, in 1938, added a selection of cloths from the Helios range. By 1938 Edinburgh Weavers' fabrics were also included in the showroom (Fig 5.8). The fabrics sold so well that members of staff at Gordon Russell Ltd began to worry that 'Wigmore Street was becoming known as a fabric rather than a furniture shop.'[19] The association between Marianne Straub and Gordon Russell Ltd — her 'first and best customer'[20] — continued through Warners, who supplied Russell Furnishing Ltd (an independent company formed after the war with L.J. Smith as London Director) until the Warner mills closed early in the 1970s. The Murphy Radio, for whose revolutionary design Dick Russell was responsible, sported radio cloths designed by Marianne Straub and manufactured at Helios and later Warners (Fig 5.9).[21] To the observer it may appear to be a

GORDON RUSSELL LTD

Fig 5.8 A page from the Gordon Russell Ltd 'Spring Fabric' brochure, 1936, showing (clockwise from top left) 'Bamboo Grass' a Warners print by Herbert Woodman; two Edinburgh Weavers cloths; 'Falling Leaf', a Warners chintz by Marion Dorn; and an upholstery doublecloth by Marianne Straub for Holywell Mills.

17 Interview with Douglas Kitching, *op cit*. Maurice Rena, in 'How Textiles are Made' *The Studio*, vol 113, January–June 1937, p96, substantiates Kitching's view, saying that Hayes-Marshall was 'the most go-ahead buyer in London of big-store calibre'.

18 Interview with Geoffrey Dunn, *op cit*.

19 Allwood, Rosamond and Laurie, Kedrun *R.D. Russell: Marion Peplar* Inner London Education Authority, 1983, p55.

20 *Ibid* footnote no 49, p57, citing Marianne Straub. It continues '. . . and whereas other people criticised her tweeds for being too stretchy, Gordon Russell Ltd's upholsterers knew how to handle it.'

21 Dick Russell was succeeded by Eden Minns and A.F. Thwaite in the 1940s. The latter was still designing radios (employing Marianne Straub cloths from Warners) when Murphy was taken over by the Rank organisation in 1962. Marianne Straub also designed radio cloths for Ekco radios while at Warners.

point over-laboured, but participants agree that to the end of the 1950s trade in this sector of the market was a gentlemanly affair, undertaken by a 'circle of friends who helped one another.'[22] It could be said that with Warners' purchase of Helios, Marianne Straub ceased working with one member of the 'club' and began with another.

There were several factors, however, that were to make her task as designer at Warners different from that at Helios. The most noticeable, although least significant, was that she was no longer responsible for both a woven and printed range. Since both firms had supplied to many of the same customers there was no sudden break in this respect, and Warners honoured outstanding

orders for Helios designs until they were no longer required, producing a score of wovens and prints up to, in some cases, 1957 (Fig 5.10). Further, she maintained the same freedom of design with the additional facility of dyes on hand at the mill. This was one of the great attractions Warners held for her, for they could dye virtually anything exactly as she specified — and in any quantity. She also delighted in the hand weaving at Warners, commenting shortly after her arrival there, 'I look at our lovely silk fabrics and there it is, the finest fabric, finer than any powerloom has

Fig 5.9 The Murphy Radio Ltd Baffle Console Radio Receiver model 'A146C' designed by R.D. Russell in 1948, with a loudspeaker cloth of rayon and cotton by Marianne Straub.

Fig 5.10 'Goatland', a transparent curtain material made with a nuralyn warp and a fancy cotton weft to prevent warp slippage. Designed and first produced in 1938 and still in production in the mid 1950s at Warners.

yet been able to do, which still are and have been produced by hand for centuries.'[23]

A far more important factor was the change which occurred in the relationship between printed and woven fabrics, which was set into motion by a number of events in the 1950s. Up to that date modern design had been more widely available at a range of prices in woven fabrics. Printed fabrics were mainly high-priced hand-block prints employing 19th century designs or low-priced roller prints employing debased versions of various period styles. The modern screen prints were hand produced in small amounts by 'up-market' firms such as Edinburgh Weavers, Alan Walton and Warners and therefore also relatively costly. By volume, the printed textile trade was dominated by the low-priced roller-printed fabrics, which accounted for nearly one-third of Britain's manufactured exports before the war. This industry was based in Lancashire and, when it collapsed in the 1950s, the loss of such a large export market, together with the associated influx of low-priced imported cloths, caused great concern throughout the textile industry. Prior to the war, market research had been regarded with some scepticism, but by 1945 had amassed substantial evidence on design for exports.[24] Manufacturers were urged to identify their market and work to maintain it by concentrating on fewer and better designs. The export market which remained was identified as much smaller (approximately 10 per cent of the total UK manufactured exports) and mainly for higher quality cloths. Competition among manufacturers increased and many began to focus their production on different, distinct markets.

Some manufacturers of quality furnishing fabrics, such as Donald Brothers and Edinburgh Weavers, chose to concentrate on the retail trade, the sphere in which Helios had operated. They used extensive advertising campaigns, Edinburgh Weavers building on the foundations

laid by Anthony Hunt, Manager of their London showroom in the 1930s. Hunt, who became editor of *House and Garden* after the war, was as skilful and persuasive a publicist for the new style in textiles as Alastair Morton, and published widely in the two years or so before the outbreak of war. In the 1950s Edinburgh Weavers employed Misha Black to design their British Industries Fair (BIF) stands and Charles Paigne, John Farleigh, Sir Hugh Casson and Edward Bawden for their advertising. Such advertising campaigns, together with the work of the CoID and the boom in popular, design-conscious magazines (*Design* — launched in 1949 — *Everywoman, Home, Homes and Gardens, House Beautiful, Housewife, Ideal Home, Woman, Woman and Home,* and *Woman's Journal*) created a public taste which was 'growing up, becoming educated, self-reliant, knowledgeable.'[25] It also created a desire for change for which a measure of quality would be sacrificed.

Warners had chosen the alternative route open to manufacturers of woven furnishing fabrics, concentrating on the contract trade and export (Fig 5.11). Here quality of cloth was essential, in the yarn, the dyes, the designing and the weaving. Colour fastness, resistance to wear and stains, ease of cleaning, the appropriate weight and structure, all had to be considered in the design. This was a task to which Marianne Straub was eminently well suited and in the weaving of which Warners had a well earned

23 Cox, Peter (ed), *op cit*, p34. Alec Hunter also gave a paper at the conference, which accompanied an exhibition in which both Warners' designers' fabrics were included. It later travelled to Edinburgh, London and Birmingham.

24 'Design and Exports' *Art and industry* November 1945, for example, containing findings of a report by W. Crawford & Partners on factors in design which affected market exports.

25 'A Survey of Textiles', *Design,* August 1955, p19.

reputation. They advertised little except to the trade, in journals such as the *Cabinet Maker*.

The alteration of the relative prices of printed and woven fabrics further separated the retail and contract market. Medium-priced printed fabrics with a variety of rapidly-changing designs were made available through the wide-scale introduction of mechanised screen printing in the mid 1950s. The process it largely replaced was roller printing: costly to set up and therefore economical only for long production runs, and limited in vertical repeat by the size of the roller. Screens were inexpensive to make, easy to change, and allowed for large-scale designs, characteristics which had previously been the province of weaving (Fig 5.12). Printed fabrics produced by mechanised screens therefore offered the first real threat to manufacturers of high-quality woven furnishing fabrics.

Well into the 1950s this threat was held at bay

COURTESY OF WARNER & SONS LTD

Fig 5.11 Warners' BIF stand of 1953. HM Queen Elizabeth is escorted by Sir Ernest Goodale and the Rt Hon Sir Peter Thorneycroft, then President of the Board of Trade. On show are 'Aldeburgh' a cotton, rayon and wool cloth designed by Marianne Straub especially for creased drapery; a Helios print 'Tree roots' and on the chair 'Marple', by Marianne Straub.

CHRIS WILLIAMS

Fig 5.12 Changing a punched paper card on the Stäubli dobby in the Warner Mill, Braintree. The Stäublis were brought from Bolton when Warners took over Helios, so that Marianne Straub could continue to design for them.

because quality had traditionally been associated with wovens and their fine fibres — silk and handspun or, at least, 'character' yarns. Ethel Mairet among others wrote in the 1930s that good cloth began with good yarn[26] and the texture thus produced became so closely linked with craftsmanship that numerous prints were manufactured up to and during the war on textured fabrics (Fig 5.13). However, as yarn prices increased in the 1950s and public preference for 'the new' instead of 'the lasting' grew, the greater expense of quality wovens tipped the scales in favour of mechanically screen-printed fabrics. The fact that they *were* new was also an asset. By 1955 *Design* reported that '... the woven textiles are on the whole less interesting than the prints ... because their average design content has for some time been high.'[27] The new screen prints were enthusiastically greeted by design critics, tired of debating the relative merits

Fig 5.13 *The cover of the announcement of the 1939 Red Rose Guild exhibition, indicating the importance of the concept of 'quality' during the '30s and '40s. The cloth is 'Howarth' by Marianne Straub, designed in 1939 and produced until 1949 by Helios and for four years more by Warners.*

of traditional block-printed designs — 'it is impossible to imagine any period when this [type of] design could look anything but right'[28] — and debased roller-printed versions — 'so-called "modern" floral designs ... uninteresting because they lack vitality'[29] — and this further influenced the public. Those firms which chose to aim their woven products at the retail trade found themselves competing with new firms such as Heal Fabrics Ltd and Hull Traders Ltd, which led the way with their outstanding commission screen-printed designs into the 1970s. Many firms with both a woven and printed range decreased the former and increased the latter, while others, producing wovens only, simply closed. By the mid 1960s retail furnishing fabrics were mainly printed.

The contract furnishing fabric manufacturers fared better, although most, like Warners, gradually increased their print production in relation to their woven. Here quality was a necessity and the higher price of manufacture could be justified. But the wide-scale introduction of mechanised screen printing, together with increased production of modern furniture, created a demand for woven fabrics which acted as a foil — either to the pattern of a printed fabric or the shape of an architect-designed chair:

'For woven fabrics the need is not for a modern 'style' as opposed to period reproductions, etc, but for a sympathetic understanding of the material, *beginning with the yarn*. This understanding, coupled with a genuine artistic sensibility, would produce designs which could then be looked

26   Mariet, 'Handweaving in England', *op cit.*
27   'A Survey of Textiles' *op cit* p21.
28   *Ibid* p29. See also *Design* 90, p33 for further comment on the chintz this quote refers to, produced by Turnbull & Stockdale from block first cut in 1830.
29   Farr, *op cit* p84.

upon as characteristic examples of modern textile art.'[30] (Fig 5.14.)

Farr first published this plea in 1953, but as much as ten years before, in her experimental work at Helios during the war, Marianne Straub had anticipated the changing role of woven furnishing textiles. From 1950 to 1970, while yarn costs escalated rapidly, she continued to lead in the development of 'characteristic examples of modern art.' That she did so for a firm which was consciously (despite its modern textiles) stressing its production of high quality, traditional designs to secure contract orders, proved a marked contrast to her environment at Helios, a firm created solely to produce modern fabrics for the retail market.

Fig 5.14 Chair by Robin Day for Hille, 1966, covered with 'Whitford', a Marianne Straub/ Warners fabric.

In the 1950s and '60s the newly design-conscious public could identify the designers responsible for their cutlery, crockery, wallpaper, printed fabrics and furniture. Ironically, with few exceptions (such as Tibor Reich), the designers of woven fabrics became even more obscure because they survived in the contract trade, two stages removed from the public. Their most successful designs were unobtrusive essays in subtle combinations of texture and colour — the least likely to attract attention. At Warners Marianne Straub designed some fabrics produced in tens of thousands of yards, but most were purchased or used by the public without knowledge of the designer (Fig 5.15). It may be safe to say that most people have sat on or looked at a Marianne Straub fabric (or a copy), yet few but the avant-garde buyer, furniture manufacturer, or reader of SIAD yearbooks could name the designer.

One of the few exceptions was her work as part of the Festival of Britain's Festival Pattern Group, in which she and Alec Hunter represented Warners. In 1949, 26 leading British manufacturers had been invited by Mark Harland Thomas, Chief Industrial Officer of the CoID, to contribute to the development of a design theme. The idea sprang from an SIA weekend course at Ashridge during which a paper was read by Professor Kathleen Lonsdale on crystallography. When approached by Thomas, she referred him to a colleague, Dr Helen Megan of Girton College, Cambridge, who agreed to become the Group's scientific consultant. Textiles were seen to be the major area of application, although since crystal structures had a natural repeat, the project was extended to include all manufacturers who employed decorative pattern: moulded and rolled glass, wallpaper, pierced metal, laminates, carpets, plastic sheeting, linoleum, leathercloth, ceramics, lace, furniture, and wrapping paper.

The choice of manufacturers was determined by Thomas, who '... wanted most of them to be leading firms of world-wide scope, for I hope thus to promote not only good design but also successful exporting.'[31] He hoped, also, that designing from magnified natural shapes would be carried on afterwards, but few designers adopted the idea. A notable exception was Tibor Reich, who set up a textile firm with backing from R. Greg & Co, the yarn manufacturers. Throughout the mid 1950s he exploited enlarged photographs of wood, stone walls, etc to produce abstract, rhythmic patterns.[32] However, many felt that so schematic a design theme could not be imposed arbitrarily:

'... however valid it may be scientifically.... Curiously, though, in so far as they anticipated a return to abstract themes they served as a catalyst and echoed well with the shapes contemporary designs and materials were developing — Ernest Race and Robin Day, for example — though the real starting point of course was Lucienne Day's "Calyx".'[33]

Over 20 different crystal structures were explored for their pattern potential, with greater variety produced through alterations in section or method of presentation. The most popular crystal structure diagrams were haemoglobin, insulin and afwillite, the first and last of which Warners used for printed and woven designs respectively. The afwillite structure was used by Marianne Straub for 'Surrey' (Fig 5.16), a wool, cotton, and rayon tapestry Jacquard. She also designed 'Helmsley', a dobby-woven all-nylon fabric based on the crystal structure of nylon. Alec Hunter chose china clay as the basis for his Jacquard design, and supervised the design of the haemoglobin-based print.

The results of the Festival Design Group provided a background for a number of displays in the Exhibition of Science, South Kensington (where Alec Hunter's design was used for curtains) and the Dome of Discovery on the South Bank. They also formed part of the Land

Fig 5.15 A prototype chair by Eric O'Leary for Conran in the 'Artist Relates' exhibition at the Ceylon Tea Centre in 1959. The background cloths are all by Marianne Straub: (left to right) 'Munster' 'Waffle Cloth' for the American Tobacco Company headquarters, 'Broadstairs' for DRU, and 'Silverton', used in the RSA redecoration of 1960.

30   *Ibid* p85.
31   Thomas, Mark Hartland, 'Festival Pattern Group' *Design* 29/30, 1951, p20.
32   See 'Foxteur', *Design* 100, April 1957, pp46–53.
33   Correspondence with Donald Tomlinson, November 1983. 'Calyx' was designed for Heal Fabrics Ltd in 1951 and shown at The Festival of Britain.

Travelling Exhibition shown in Manchester, Birmingham, Leeds and Nottingham. The centrepiece for the promotion of the project was the Regatta Restaurant, reserved for this purpose by the designer, Misha Black. He selected Marianne Straub's 'Welland' (a dobby-woven all-nylon upholstery cloth) for the chair coverings and her 'Surrey' for large expanses of curtaining (Fig 5.17). As a result it was the most prominent feature of the Festival Design Group and naturally became the best known of her designs in the 1950s, although it is not representative of her

work of the period. Like many of the other objects produced through this scheme, it was never mass-produced.

'Surrey' is more appropriately regarded as the tip of the iceberg. During her 20 years at Warners, Marianne Straub put, on average, 100 warps a year on her hand looms, most of which were used by the designer to evolve several variations of a design (Fig 5.18). Ironically, the success of some designs, together with the trend in the textile industry towards smaller ranges, meant that a good proportion of her designs never went into production. In all, perhaps 300–400 were used, although many of these were re-coloured or re-worked in a different weight at a later date for a specific client.

Heal Fabrics Ltd (HFL) provides a typical example. It was formed at the instigation of Tom Worthington, director of Heal's Wholesalers and Export Ltd (created in 1941, initially to use surplus war materials). In 1946 textiles began to be supplied through HFL and, as was true of

Fig 5.16 'Surrey' by Marianne Straub for the festival of Britain. Jacquard-woven in wool, cotton and rayon, it was used in the Regatta Restaurant in dark green, gold and white.

Fig 5.17 The Regatta Restaurant, designed by Misha Black. 'Surrey' can be seen covering large expanses on the first floor. Race Antelope chairs can be seen on the ground floor.

most furniture makers and all wholesale firms, they required manufacturers to give them exclusive rights to a design. Although HFL rapidly became known for its printed textiles range, they also wholesaled avant-garde wovens. Among these were one woven design a year between 1954 and 1961 from Warners, most running for several years (Fig 5.19). Six of these designs were by Marianne Straub, regarded by HFL staff as a 'flexible, sound and prolific designer'.[34] N.J. Colgate, who joined HFL in 1946, transferred to Woolland's for two years in the mid 1950s and during that time also visited the designer in her studio at the Braintree mill, where:

'. . . she would produce boxes of samples which we would pore over, enthusiastically discussing variations which could be introduced to obtain a slightly different effect.'[35]

'Munster', a dobby-woven cloth with a black cotton warp and a knicker wool and gimp weft, was chosen by Tom Worthington for HFL in 1957 and stocked in eight colours. In 1961 and 1967 the turquoise version was re-worked because yarns became unavailable, the only two tasks which Marianne Straub performed for HFL in the last ten years of her employment at Warners — not because the cloth didn't sell, but

Fig 5.18 Marianne Straub in her Braintree studio in 1961.

34   Interview with N.J. Colgate, 11 October 1983.
35   *Op cit.* Colgate returned to HFL in 1956 and became director on Tom Worthington's death. On the closure of HFL in 1983 he purchased part of the range and with it formed Ambrose Fabrics.

because it *did*. It was woven by Warners until January 1971, during which time over 500 000 yards were produced. Under ideal conditions this represents the total output of three looms producing 62 yards a day, 250 days a year, for 11 years. In fact, the orders gradually increased so that they occupied six or seven looms full-time during the last three years of production. The bulk of the fabric was contracted by HFL to the Ministry of Works, and chairs covered with it are still in use today (Fig 5.20).[36]

Like HFL, Parker Knoll Textiles (now Parkertex Fabrics) held exclusive rights to one or two Warner fabrics at a time. Parker Knoll Textiles was set up by Douglas Kitching at the invitation of Parker Knoll Furniture in 1950. Kitching brought to his position as Managing Director a knowledge of the textile trade gained during his years with Warners and Helios, and nine of the twelve Warner fabrics confined to Parker Knoll Textiles between 1953 and 1965 were designed by Marianne Straub (Fig 5.21). Most of these were also used by the parent company on their furniture. One, 'Armure', was produced in 18 colours over a period of ten years.[37] The standard which Douglas Kitching set for Parker Knoll Textiles was high, for each cloth was sold with a guarantee of good faith that the weaving was sound. He knew Marianne Straub's designs met this standard:

> 'One of the problems with textile design is [that] if you're an upholsterer you must have something that is going to wear. If you're a designer you can get better effect by having longer floats . . . and the ones we liked best of Marianne's were those that gave the best of both. In other words they were well

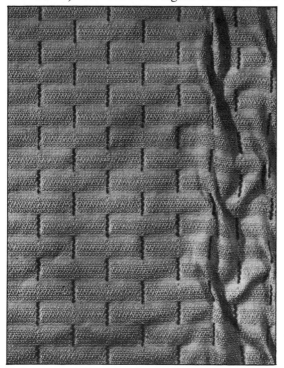

Fig 5.19 One of the first fabrics designed by Marianne Straub at Warners. It was stocked by Heals and still covers the designer's own early 1950s Race sofa (see Fig 7.4).

DRU/PHOTO MALTBY

Fig 5.20 A flat in the 'Oriana' designed by Ian Hodgson of R.D. Russell and Partners; the furniture is covered in 'Munster'.

bound in and yet they were interesting in design. The two things don't often go together.[38]

In addition to her contacts from Helios days and her own work as 'sales rep', Marianne Straub's acceptance among the small circle of avant-garde designers led to introductions to prospective customers such as Lucienne Ercolani, who was first employed as a furniture designer in 1910 by Harry Parker of Frederick Parker (now Parker Knoll) and remained in contact with the company. Having developed the solid wood (beech

and elm) Ercol Windsor furniture successfully from the first group made for the 'Britain Can Make It' exhibition,[39] he came to Kitching early in the 1950s with a particular cloth in mind. Kitching immediately recognised the design problems as one which Marianne Straub could solve. Shortly afterwards he set up a meeting between the two designers and the resulting

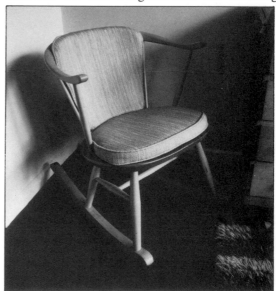

Fig 5.22 A nursing chair by Lucienne Ercolani with its original cushion covered with 'Carlton', a cotton and worsted dobby-woven cloth designed by Marianne Straub in 1959.

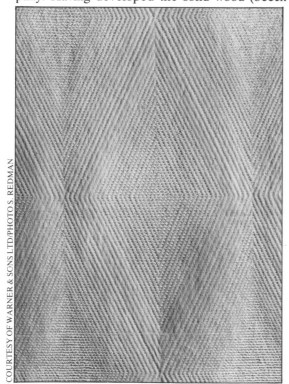

COURTESY OF WARNER & SONS LTD/PHOTO S. REDMAN

Fig 5.21 'Downton', a Jacquard-woven cotton, fibre and gimp cloth designed by Marianne Straub for Parker Knoll in 1956.

36 At Addenbrooke's Hospital in Cambridge, for example. Information on yardage, colourways, etc is derived from samples, production records and design books held in the Warner Archive. The design books are complete.
37 'Armure' was specifically designed for use on the outside of a chair with a tapestry seat and inner back (eg the Penshurst chair in Fareham tapestry, circa 1952).
38 Interview with Douglas Kitching, *op cit.*
39 See Ercolani, Lucian R. *A Furniture Maker* Ernest Benn Ltd, 1975, for an account of the development of Windsor furniture.

fabrics were woven at Warners and sold to Ercolani through Parker Knoll Textiles (Fig 5.22). By coincidence, in the interim Marianne Straub was introduced to Ercolani by George Breeze, buyer for Lewis's Provincial Stores and a friend of Margaret Pilkington's sister, Dorothy. One of Ercolani's assistants, Fritz Muller, had been a salesman under L.J. Smith in Gordon Russell's London showroom (40 Wigmore Street) and was therefore also acquainted with Marianne Straub's Welsh tweeds and Helios fabrics. Ercolani also had fabrics consigned to him from Heal Fabrics Ltd, among them Marianne Straub's 'Russell Check' and, in the latter years of the 1950s, special colourings of the 'Munster'.

A number of fabrics, including 'Broadstairs' were commissioned by Misha Black of the Design Research Unit, most for ships such as the SS 'Oriana' (Fig 5.23), launched on 3 December

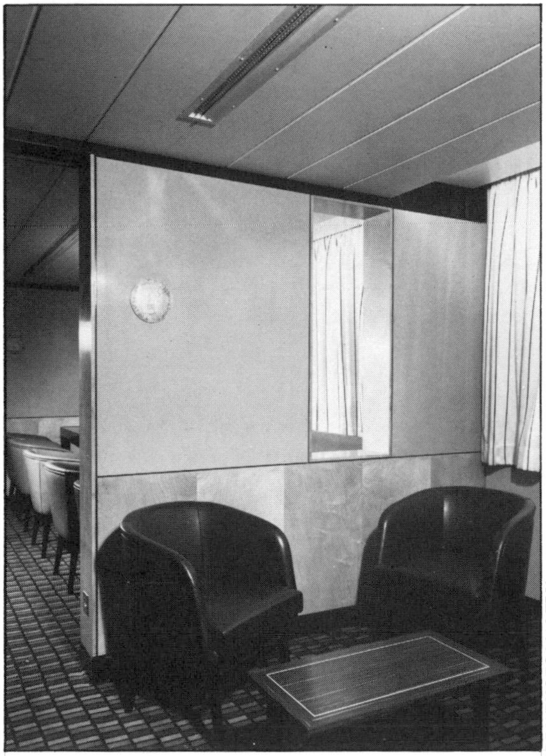

DRU/PHOTO MALTBY

Fig 5.23 The Silver Grill aboard the SS 'Oriana', curtains ('Barfield') designed by Marianne Straub for the Design Research Unit.

DRU/PHOTO HEINZ ZINRAM

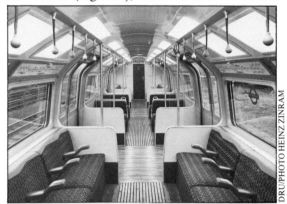

Fig 5.24 The new Victoria line, 1968, with upholstery described as 'old-style moquette' (designer unknown).

DRU/PHOTO HEINZ ZINRAM

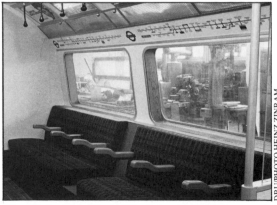

Fig 5.24a The Piccadilly Line prototype showing the Marianne Straub moquette originally designed in 1964 for the Victoria Line.

1960. The seemingly ubiquitous 'Munster' (see Fig 5.20) was also used by the DRU in this ship as part of the interiors designed by the Russell partnership, who were responsible for the 1st class restaurant, 1st and tourist class cabins, and crew and officers quarters. In 1964 Marianne Straub designed an upholstery fabric intended for the DRU's new Victoria Line underground train, but instead London Transport chose to use an 'old style moquette'.[40] The cloth she had designed was eventually used in several other London underground train lines (the first, the Piccadilly, in 1976) and on London Transport buses (Figs 5.24 & 5.24a). The two designers worked together in other capacities, initially as external examiners in Scotland. It was Misha Black who put Marianne Straub forward for the SIA in 1945 and they served together on the SIAD International Relations Committee, Misha Black as Chairman, Marianne Straub as Secretary. She was also Chairman of the SIAD Fashion and Textile Groups from 1953 to 1955. Through these professional contacts Marianne Straub developed great admiration for Misha Black, both in his work and the unassuming way in which he went about it.

The long association between Gordon Russell Ltd and Marianne Straub has already been noted, and her fabrics were among those used by R.D. Russell in his private (post-war) practice. When he redesigned the interior of the Grosvenor House Burghley Room in 1961 his wife, Marian Peplar, worked with him as she often did as consultant on colour and textiles. She selected, among others, one of Marianne Straub's fabrics for the chairs. Mrs Russell recalls that she and her husband admired Marianne Straub 'as a very warm and lively minded person, and a designer of great integrity.'[41] Marianne Straub's association with Gordon Russell Ltd extended to the independent contract furnishing company, Russell Furnishing Ltd (RFL), estab-

lished in 1947 with L.J. Smith as Director.[42] He first met Marianne Straub in 1938 when Sir Thomas Barlow brought her to 40 Wigmore Street, where Smith was Manager. After she joined Warners, Smith frequently discussed projects with her and '. . . took her ideas because she knew much more about it.'[43] During the same period RFL was buying Welsh tweeds (designed 10–15 years earlier by Marianne Straub) in bulk. These were used in pubs and the many university hostel blocks that were being built in the 1950s and '60s, the first of which RFL re-furnished at Kings College, Newcastle. L.J. Smith regarded Marianne Straub's Welsh tweeds as 'faultless' and had a very high regard for her skill as a designer:

'She had this wonderful aptitude which you only find in first class designers . . . she had a natural instinct for the material in which she was working — like a first-class potter or cabinet-maker. There was nothing superficial about it, she had a *depth* of feeling for the material and the way it should be used. She'd sell the thing for us before you could say Jack Robinson!'[44]

Russell Furnishing Ltd operated for 23 years, throughout calling on Marianne Straub for assistance. 'Broadfield', designed in 1954, was confined to RFL and used shortly afterwards in ICI's Midland office. Many fabrics began as a

40 'Views and Reviews' *Architectural Review,* November 1968, p385. I am indebted to Frederick Dickenson for information regarding the past work of the DRU.

41 Correspondence from Marian Russell, 17 February 1984.

42 E.T. Ould and R.H. Bee were co-directors from Gordon Russell Ltd; Smith was controlling Director for Russell Furnishing Ltd.

43 Interview with L.J. Smith, 26 October 1983.

44 *Ibid.* I am also indebted to Trevor Chinn of Gordon Russell Ltd for information on and illustrations of Marianne Straub's work.

result of a specific project, to be used again if required. For the architects Jackson & Edmonds (of Birmingham and Welbeck Street, London), special stage curtains were made for Bury's new Town Hall in 1950 and for the Chelmsford Civic Centre in about 1964. In 1969 she designed fabrics for three Stratford-upon-Avon projects undertaken by HFL, including Anne Hathaway's Cottage and the Shakespeare Theatre. They employed natural fibres and colouring: 'Romeo' all linen, 'Juliet' bleached and scoured worsted, and 'Hathaway' Welsh S-spun Craftsman's Mark yarn. In designing them Marianne Straub relied on her wide knowledge of handweaving, spinning and dyeing. These were her only cloths produced by the hand-weavers at Warners.

The Stratford cloths were not for mass-production and this was one of the advantages of Warners, which would produce as little as 20

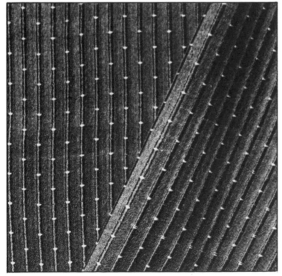

Fig 5.25 'Marple Spot' designed by Marianne Straub in 1952 on the same warp as 'Marple' (see Fig 5.11). Both cloths were principally fibro with a 'raised' warp stripe of cotton.

yards of one design. More typical were the cloths 'Silverton' (1952, one of the first mass-produced cloths to use Lurex), 'Antique Satin', 'Marple' and 'Marple Spot' (Fig 5.25), which were among the few fabrics sold in volume directly by Warners. Ideal for public use, they were taken in large amounts by exporters and the Ministry of Works who, for example, ordered 28 000 yards of Marianne Straub's 'Lydney' (a worsted and cotton cloth) in 1964. Her fabrics employed subtle combinations of colour and yarn which often relied on variable-spaced reeding to create narrow vertical stripes of different density and width. These are examples of Marianne Straub's ability to produce interesting textiles which were easy to weave once set up. To her, this type of designing was:

'. . . a good form of lateral thinking, because you had to think of cost, you had to think of feasibility of production, you always had to think that the weavers were on piece rate so if you made something which was very difficult you could run into trouble there. You had to think of colour fastness, you had to think of wear tests — later on very much so when the rubbing test became important — and flammability, all the things which come in particularly when you design for public use. Finally, the result had to be aesthetically acceptable.'[45]

Among the special projects which Marianne Straub undertook for Warners were cinema curtains for the American Embassy in London, designed in consultation with the architect, Saarinen; fabrics for Canadian Pacific's 'Empress of Canada'; re-design of Albert Swindell's utility cloth ('Frinton') for British Rail's London Midland region carriages in the early 1950s (Fig 5.26); fabrics for Guildford Cathedral in 1954; upholstery cloth ('Shaded Stripe') for the Birmingham Railway Carriage Company in

Fig 5.26 'Finton' upholstery in two colourways as reworked by Marianne Straub for British Rail from Albert Swindell's utility-standard cloth, early 1950s.

Fig 5.27 The Warner High Voltage Screening Suit in use by CEGB staff. The worsted cloth contained fine stainless steel thread at ¼ inch intervals in both warp and weft.

1959; curtains for the Carlton Towers, London in 1966; upholstery cloth ('Gemini') and sheer leno curtaining ('Pisces') for the redecoration of the London Hilton Rooftop Restaurant in 1967; and a worsted cloth incorporating flexible fine stainless steel thread conducting filaments for a high-voltage screening suit in 1968 (Fig 5.27). However, as her work for Heals Fabrics Ltd, Parker Knoll Textiles and Russell Furnishing Ltd indicates, most of Marianne Straub's mass-produced designs were sold through other whole-salers, this often making the identification of the end-user difficult. Typical are the several cloths designed for the wholesale division of Libertys, one of which, 'Aleppo', was included in the British show-flat at the Halsingborg Exhibition in Sweden in 1955 (Fig 5.28).

The Warner range in the 1950s and '60s continued to show traditional woven designs side-by-side with modern designs, including many boldly patterned Jacquards by Frank Davies, who joined the firm in 1951 after studying at the Birmingham College of Art and the Royal College of Art. Alec Hunter, as production manager, had overall control over the range, but did fewer woven designs after his appointment to the Board of Directors in 1943. After 1950 his greater influence was on the printed range and, at his instigation, four artist-designed prints were produced in 1957 ('Cherubs' by Lytton Lamb, 'House of Cards' by Milner Grey, 'Olympus' by Edward Bawden, and 'San Marco' by James Fitton) (Fig 5.29). In 1957 he became President of the SIA, which further drew him away from active involvement in the wovens design department. He had, in any case, envisioned that Marianne Straub would work in the same independent way that Theo Moorman had — as a separate, more experimen-tal design department[46] — and therefore left her

CENTRAL ELECTRICITY RESEARCH LABORATORIES

45 Marianne Straub. The weavers were paid by the pick.

THE COTTON BOARD

Fig 5.28 A Cotton Board Colour Design & Style Centre exhibition, c1956, showing SIA members' work. Marianne Straub's 'Aleppo' (shown in the British show flat in Sweden shortly before) is centre right. In the foreground is 'Encore' furniture by Howard Keith and an Axminster rug by Tibor Reich for Quayle & Tranter Ltd.

very much to her own devices. This was a freedom which she appreciated, although she was aware that her stylistic 'distance' from the Warner range made it difficult for the salesmen to show her fabrics to clients already certain that they knew the Warner handwriting.[47] To a large extent, therefore, her designs remained unexploited by Warners; her function was less as a designer for their range and more as one for their looms.

In 1956 Marianne Straub began teaching part-time, thereafter only working in her Braintree studio two or three days a week, except during the academic holidays when she returned to full-time designing. Despite this her designs occupied a large proportion of Warner's powerloom production, seldom falling below 50 per cent and reaching a peak of 90 per cent in 1968. Most of this was accounted for by the weaving of 'Munster' for the Ministry of Works and of various cloths for Tamesa Fabrics, with whom she did most of her collaborative designing at Warners between 1963 and her retirement late in November 1970.

Fig 5.29 James Fitton's 'San Marco' (left) and Lytton Lamb's 'Cherubs', two of several artist-designed prints commissioned by Alec Hunter for Warners in 1957, with 'Silverton' by Marianne Straub.

46   Marianne Straub's studio at Warners contained two dobbies, a 12-shaft countermarch Lervad and a 16-shaft countermarch.
47   At the Dartington Hall conference (Cox, *op cit* p34) Gordon Russell remarked 'I think, knowing something of Marianne Straub's problems, that she will tell you that the education of the salesman is much more difficult than the education of the worker in the mill, who has some feeling for material. To my mind there is no hope until you get over this problem of selling things through people who really know what the thing itself is. If you distribute things more generally you only get the kind of thing that you see in the ordinary arts and crafts shops.'

Tamesa

In January 1964 Isabel Tisdall launched Tamesa Fabrics. Her aim was to commission 'very special weaves'[1] and to cater to the exclusive market which was increasingly buying expensive wovens from the continent. Behind her she had seven years at Edinburgh Weavers as stylist responsible for the re-launch of the company and more years as a fashion editor with *Vogue.* She not only knew the field but was able to assess likely rivals with a critical journalist's eye. As a result Tamesa Fabrics specialised in a small collection of 'exotic and original'[2] weaves, their luxury derived from subtle contrasts in texture and tone (Fig 5.30). This was supplemented by a handful of printed fabrics, most designed by her husband, Hans Tisdall, an artist whose textile designs had been widely used by Edinburgh Weavers as well as Warners and Helios.

Fig 5.30 A detail of Marianne Straub's hand-woven prototype of 'Oriel', 1969, employing bleached worsted with Rexor Meton Gold thread.

From the outset Isabel Tisdall commissioned the printing and weaving from Warners and, by 1968, Tamesa production occupied between 15 and 20 dobby looms full-time and one or two Jacquard looms. Isabel Tisdall chose to discuss her projected range with Warners in 1963 because she '. . . knew Marianne Straub's work and very much admired it.'[3] Marianne Straub and Isabel Tisdall had already been introduced to each other briefly by Alastair Morton, and Hans Tisdall was known by reputation to Marianne Straub through his contact with Mr Loewenstein regarding designs for Helios. The success of their first meeting was, however, largely based on Isabel Tisdall's immediate realisation that she had found a designer sensitive to those qualities on which she was determined to base her reputation: 'subtle and sophisticated colour combinations and reserved richness in texture and sheen'.[4] Marianne Straub, in return, recognised the discrimination with which Mrs Tisdall discussed her fabrics.

The first collection included 'Echo Check', 'Echo Stripe', 'Umbria', and 'Assisi' (Fig 5.31). It was greeted with great enthusiasm:

> 'Mrs Tisdall has marshalled an impressive array of prints and weaves all designed by a small panel of designers for the Tamesa label. The weaves employ cotton, rayon, linen, wool and silk individually and in combination to produce some luxurious drapes dyed in natural and sombre tones that provide refreshing relief from the strident colour of many modern furnishing fabrics.'[5]

It was not a large collection 'but of excellent quality',[6] which appealed particularly to architects and designers — essentially a contract rather than a retail range. The first major order (for 'Umbria') was placed by architect Howard Kenton. At the Design Research Unit (DRU), the consortium of architects and designers headed by Milner Grey and Misha Black took note, consistently commenting in their in-house bulletin as each new Tamesa collection appeared. While they found at Edinburgh Weavers (recently merged with Morton Sundour at their takeover by Courtaulds in 1963, the year of Alastair Morton's death) that 'the glory seems to have departed',[7] that Tibor Reich's fabrics were reasonably priced but 'pretty ordinary'[8] and

Fig 5.31 Fabrics in the new Tamesa showroom in Kings Road, London, showing a dark-ground 'Echo Check' in the foreground. 'Echo Check' was originally designed by Marianne Straub in 1962.

that another manufacturer's product was '. . . not likely to be of use to us, unless we are designing millionaires boudoirs or barbeque pits',[9] Tamesa's woven range contained 'excellent new fabrics, very rich textures' and 'lovely quality and colours' in their 'beautifully shown small collection'.[10] Members of the DRU were urged to visit the showrooms of Tamesa to appreciate the cloths, shown there in simply displayed sweeping lengths. 'Echo Stripe' was a particular favourite at the DRU, where its designer was already well known and '. . . greatly admired, both [for] her work and the tremendous spirit with which she . . . promoted improvement in the quality of woven textile design.'[11]

In general, Tamesa introduced five or six new weaves into each new range, which appeared annually when Isabel Tisdall was satisfied that the collection read well as a whole. The woven fabrics of the first 8–10 years of Tamesa's existence are particularly important as the clearest indication of Marianne Straub's own tastes, forming the 'backbone' of the range she would have produced at Helios had it been functioning during these years. Contributing to Tamesa's success was therefore extremely satisfying, especially when developing fabrics in conjunction with the architect or designer, working slowly and selectively with Isabel Tisdall, who

1   *Design* 237 p34.
2   *Ibid.*
3   Telephone interview with Isabel Tisdall, 24 October 1983.
4   *Design* 237, *op cit* p34.
5   *Design* 194, February 1965, p60.
6   Design Research Unit *Bulletin*, February 1965 (in-house publication).
7   Design Research Unit *Bulletin*, October 1966.
8   Design Research Unit *Bulletin*, October 1965.
9   Design Research Unit *Bulletin*, November 1968.
10 Design Research Unit *Bulletin*, respectively: March 1966, March 1968 and November 1971.
11 Correspondence from Sir Milner Gray, 9 January 1984.

took samples from the mill to the client until the colour, texture and weight were exactly suited to their eventual setting (Fig 5.32).

Fabrics were also stocked which could be piece dyed to the client's specifications. Certain ranges were especially suited to large buildings and, in several cases (such as 'Copellia', designed in 1968), one design would be woven in seven or eight different colours to be used by architects to distinguish different functional areas of a building. Universities and libraries figured large among Tamesa clients, due to the up-grading and expansion of existing institutions and the creation of seven new universities in the 1960s. One of the first such projects for which Tamesa supplied fabrics was York University library, in which 'Echo Check' was hung. In 1968 Marianne

Straub designed the first of several blankets for Tamesa which were destined for use in a number of university hostels (Fig 5.33).

'Echo Check' and 'Echo Stripe' were created as a quartet based on two colours, each colour used as the basis for the plain-effect cloth, 'Stripes', and in dark-on-light and light-on-dark combinations in the 'Checks'. Such a quartet in caramel and white was used by Jo Pattrick in the decoration of the officers' rooms in the 'QE2' in 1968, and throughout the second half of the 1960s this range was a top export to Sweden, Holland and Italy (Fig 5.34). Tamesa also supplied other fabrics to the 'QE2', all designed by Marianne Straub. 'Visor', designed in 1966 (Fig 5.35), was used by Jon Bannenberg in his designs for the deluxe cabins and the first class restau-

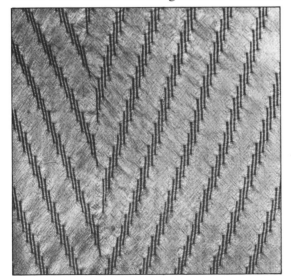

Fig 5.32 A detail of 'Coppelia', an all-worsted curtaining cloth designed by Marianne Straub in 1967. The impact of the very large scale herringbone motif is emphasised by the distortion which occurs between plain and patterned areas.

Fig 5.33 Tamesa blankets, 1969, designed by Marianne Straub. Among all of the fabrics designed between 1963 and 1970 by Marianne Straub for Tamesa, only the blankets were not originally produced by Warner & Sons Ltd.

rant; 'Columbia', designed by Dennis Lennon, employed 'Tamesa Star', a plain weave cloth of 100 per cent spun rayon.[12] Unusual in a range which emphasised natural fibres, its drape and sheen made it a popular substitute for silk fabrics at a time when silk was in short supply throughout the world, and it became one of Tamesa's best sellers. It was originally sampled in 1964 on 13 rayon warps of different colours, each woven with a selection of 18 different coloured wefts of viscose slub to create over 150 different colourways. Later more colour trials were done, to total 301 in all. Of these, 30 were put into the Tamesa range. Marianne Straub's skill as a colourist is evident in plain cloths such as 'Tamesa Star', for they relied on the combination of two colours for their rich, luxurious appearance.

An unexpected silky sheen was also a characteristic of the closely woven all-worsted co-ordinated trio, 'Venus', 'Aries', and 'Leo', designed by Marianne Straub for Tamesa in 1967. These subtle, textural cloths were selected to provide related fabrics in different weights for curtains, bedspreads and upholstery. These too, were used on the 'QE2': 'Venus' in the lounge designed by Michael Inchbald and the trio of fabrics in the luxury suites by Dennis Lennon. 'Aurora', a light, open-weave cloth, was also employed on the ship (Fig 5.36). Constructed of cotton and viscose slub with vertical stripes created by spaced reeding, 'Aurora' was originally designed by Marianne Straub for Tamesa's redecoration of the British Embassy in Paris in 1965.

ARCAID/BRECHT-EINZIG

Fig 5.34 The Officers' Dining Room on the 'QE2', designed by Jo Pattrick. The far wall is curtained with an off-white ground 'Echo Check'.

12 Warner silk was used in the Grill Room and Bar designed by Dennis Lennon & Partners, who co-ordinated the entire scheme. Geoffrey Dunn, as advisor on the design and manufacture of all free-standing furniture for Cunard Lines, was also involved in the planning of the QE2 interiors.

Other cloths which were designed by Marianne Straub for particular Tamesa projects include 'Concerto', a heavy textured cloth of wool, worsted and Tussor silk for the Queen Elizabeth Hall (designed by Herbert Bennett and completed in 1967); upholstery fabric for the British Airways Trident and curtain material for British Rail's Midland region trains. A handful of the wovens were stocked by retail shops such as Heals, which had 'Score' and 'Visor' in their range from 1966 to 1969 and 'Aurora' from 1970 to 1973. The Tamesa range also included a small number of bold geometric Jacquards designed by Frank Davies of Warners and a range of imported sheers and wallcoverings.

The combination of Isabel Tisdall's awareness of the needs of her clients with Marianne Straub's design skills created a sound basis for the expansion of Tamesa Fabrics, which succeeded in capturing a wide export market within its first four years of operation. By its twelfth year, 1976, Tamesa was able to open a branch in Brussels. Much of the cloth had been woven in Belgium since the closure of the Warner mills in March 1971, although the hand screen-printing and woollen and linen weaving was still carried out in the UK. Marianne Straub continued to design for Tamesa until 1975, although she had retired from Warners five years before. Several of the cloths which she created for Isabel Tisdall while at Warners continued in the Tamesa range well into the 1970s and 'Aurora' and 'Flair' remain there today, having been in demand for 19 and 12 years respectively (Fig 5.37).

Fig 5.35 'Visor', 1966, a 100% cotton (dyed and undyed) curtaining fabric designed by Marianne Straub for Tamesa in three colourways; peat, beige and bronze. The latter colourway was used in the 'QE2'.

Fig 5.36 'Aurora', designed in 1965. The cloth is a plain weave (the weft of undyed viscose slub, the warp of undyed mercerised cotton) with the pattern effect derived entirely from spaced reeding.

Left: A private residence with fabrics designed between 1940 and 1965 by Marianne Straub: cushions for Helios, upholstery fabric for Warners (sofa 'Munster' 1957, chair 'Chandos' 1960), and curtains for Tamesa ('Echo Stripe' 1964). Below left: Another contemporary interior showing Helios curtains ('Elgin' 1938) and lampshade ('Goathland' 1949), Warners cushion covers ('Aldeburgh' 1953) and a Tamesa tablecloth ('Echo Check' 1964). Below right: 'Norwich', originally designed by Marianne Straub for Helios. Also produced by Warners and, in 1982, by Devere Mill for Thaxted's Morris dancers' waistcoats.

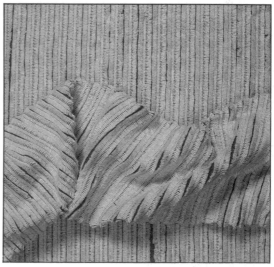

Previous page

A scarf of undyed Southdown wool and natural-dyed eri silk woven by Marianne Straub at Gospels, 1933, together with five samples showing her supplementary weft and doublecloth techniques. The backgrounds are (left) Welsh doublecloth exclusive to Gordon Russell Ltd, designed by Marianne Straub and woven at Holywell textile mill, c1936; and (right) silk and wool doublecloth woven by Marianne Straub while at Gospels. The right-hand page shows (above) five dress-weight Welsh tweeds and (below) four upholstery-weight Welsh doublecloths, all designed by Marianne Straub, 1934–7.

This page (from right)

A selection of Helios fabrics, the dobby- and Jacquard-woven fabrics designed by Marianne Straub, the two prints selected by her for inclusion in the range: 'Wynchwood' (Noldi Soland c1939), 'Hastings' (1937), 'St Pierre' (1937), 'Mercury' (1938), 'Perth' (1939), 'Grange (1939), 'Somerby' (1940), 'Epping' (Marianne Mahler c1940), 'Ascot' (1938), 'Muncaster' (1946), 'Griesdale' (1946), 'Goathland' (1949), 'St Mary' (1937) and 'St Hilier' (1937).

Warner fabrics by Marianne Straub (from right): 'Broadfield' (Design Research Unit 1952), 'Silverton' (Warners 1952), 'Colbury' (Warners 1964), 'Munster' (HFL 1957), 'Russell Check' (Ercol Furniture 1955), 'Tangier' (Parker Knoll 1960), 'Chandos' (HFL and Ercol Furniture 1960), 'Gemini' (Hilton Rooftop Restaurant 1968), and seven Warners fabrics for Tamesa: 'Jupiter', 'Aires' (for British Rail Southern Region 1966), 'Checkmate' (1968) and 'Victor' (1967) by Marianne Straub; 'Allegro' (1968) by Frank Davies; and 'Umbria' (1964) and 'Cheney' (1970) by Marianne Straub.

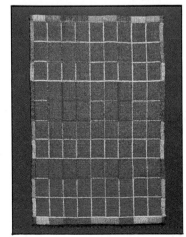

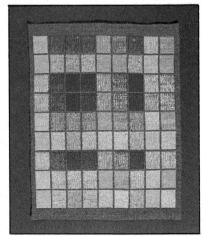

Top: 'Four panels' (each approx. 240 × 90 cm) designed by Marianne Straub for the Huddersfield Central Services building in 1977.
Below: Two of Marianne Straub's experimental worsted and Chinese silk doublecloth hangings (each approx. 50 × 35 cm), spring 1983.

Fig 5.37 A detail of a hand-woven prototype variation of 'Flair' originally designed by Marianne Straub for Tamesa shortly after her retirement from Warners in November 1970. The pattern of staggered rectangles forms a 'chequerboard' overall.

Great Bardfield Artists

Throughout her life Marianne Straub responded positively to a challenging and stimulating environment; during her years at Warners this was provided in Great Bardfield, her home in Essex from 1953 to 1970. Here a group of artists was based who had gradually come together from 1932, when Edward Bawden and Eric Ravilious settled in the village. With Bawden and Ravilious's reputations well established a decade later, the Council for the Encouragement of Museums and Arts organised an exhibition of 'Great Bardfield Painters', which then included Kenneth Rowntree, Geoffrey Rhodes, Michael Rothenstein and John Aldridge. Shortly after the war both amateur and professional painters in the parish were invited to exhibit in the local town hall. When Great Bardfield was sponsored by the Essex Rural Community Council as one of three Festival of Britain villages in 1951, residents were called upon to produce a similar exhibition, this time dispayed in their own homes. The success of the 1951 exhibition led to a further exhibition in 1954, different in that only the professional artists of the village participated. In this year only three of the 'founder' members remained — Bawden, Aldridge, and Rothenstein — and six others had arrived: George Chapman, Walter Hoyle, S. Clifford-Smith, Audrey Cruddas, David Lowe and Marianne Straub.

Marianne Straub had been introduced to the Bawdens through mutual friends shortly after her move to Braintree in 1950 and recalls going both to Great Bardfield to see the Festival exhibition and with Walter Hoyle to nearby Thaxted to see the Morris Dancers, one of whom was Alec Hunter. Throughout 1951 she was frequently in Great Bardfield where, like herself, many of the artists there were preparing contributions to the Festival of Britain, most notably Bawden, who designed the mural for the Lion and Unicorn pavilion. The same pavilion contained the work of a lesser known craftsman,

Fred Misen, gardener to the Bawdens and the Aldridges. It was Misen who made the large wheat straw lion and unicorn 'corn-dollies' and whose work was to be seen in most of the Bardfield artists' homes. Marianne Straub's purchase of the thatched Trinity Cottage in Great Bardfield's high street (Fig 5.38) late in 1952 came about:

'. . . through the Festival of Britain . . . when I went over a lot and I decided it would be a nice place to live. One day Edward Bawden rang and said "My gardener says the cottage opposite is for sale", so I drove over and looked at the cottage and decided to buy it.'[1]

Thus Marianne Straub took up residence at Trinity Cottage in January 1953, joining the Great Bardfield artists for their most noted

Fig 5.38 The back of Marianne Straub's Great Bardfield cottage, 1956.

period. During the 1954 exhibition her work (together with Walter Hoyle's) was shown at the Bawden's, but the success of the open house prompted an exhibition in the following year, for which her house was also opened to the public. The 1955 exhibition was organised on a much larger scale, with posters and catalogues. The result was a staggering increase in attendance[2]

and a promise that the group would continue to exhibit annually. In fact, the group were to hold only one further open house exhibition, in 1958, although a small travelling exhibition was circulated in 1957, by which time two further artists, Sheila Robinson and Bernard Cheese, had joined those already in Great Bardfield and one, the cartoonist David Lowe, had left.

Fig 5.39 Michael Rothenstein's studio, in Great Bardfield, mid 1950s (left to right) Walter Hoyle, Marianne Straub and students.

1   Taped interview (no 1) with Marianne Straub.
2   Accounts at the time estimate an increase from 1700 visitors in 1954 to over 6000 in 1955; this was greatly facilitated by special buses from the train station.

Despite the brevity of the formal activities of the artists in Great Bardfield, the friendships remained active, particularly among the Bawdens, Walter Hoyle, Sheila Robinson, the Chapmans, the Aldridges and Marianne Straub (Fig 5.39). The Bawdens' daughter, Joanne, had spent nine months threading up looms for Marianne Straub at Warners in 1952 prior to studying weaving at the Royal College of Art.

She and Marianne Straub were therefore friends from the pre-Bardfield days and they too remained so. As members of the artists' 'colony' moved away from Bardfield (likened to Montmartre by one reporter) they maintained contact and, since they had been brought together by geography rather than style, there was no apparent change in their work. During the four years (1955–58) in which the exhibitions were widely

Fig 5.40 Edward Bawden in the living room of his Great Bardfield home, surrounded by his own work, including the 'Periwinkle' wallpaper by Coles, and the work of his friends: Ravillious mugs, Lucie Aldridge hooked rug, Barron & Larcher cushion cover, and Marianne Straub loose furniture covers.

reported, the Bardfield artists were at pains to stress their diversity. However, closer study reveals some similarities in application rather than appearance — in their 'strong workmanlike bias towards the decorative arts.'[3] Bawden's contribution to industrial design is well documented[4] and the 1955 Great Bardfield exhibition included a wide selection of his work, ranging from cast-iron furniture to beer bottle labels and wallpapers. He began designing wallpapers in the mid 1930s and, together with Aldridge, produced the 'Bardfield' wallpaper collection in 1938 for Coles (Fig 5.40). Although this was Aldridge's only sojourn from painting, all the other painters in the group had at one time practised an applied art. Hoyle, too, designed for Coles, as well as for Sandersons and the Wallpaper Manufacturers Ltd. Chapman had been a graphic designer before the war and Clifford-Smith a carpet designer. The latter, together with his wife, the textile designer Joan Glass, had produced hand blocked-printed textiles during the war. Rothenstein is also recorded as designing wallpapers. With Audrey Cruddas (a painter turned theatrical designer), Bernard Cheese (a painter and graphics designer), his wife, Sheila Robinson (a poster and advertising designer), and Marianne Straub, the group achieved a balance between the fine and applied arts. A contemporary commentator concluded that:

'. . . the dreadful divorce between "the artist and society" does not seem to have afflicted these gifted men and women in the slightest . . . each of these artists has discovered positive means of adapting his talents to the practical demands of the public, without any loss of artistic integrity whatever.'[5]

A second factor which united the group was their appreciation of each other's work, so that within any one artist's home could be found the work of most of the others. For example, Marianne

Straub's house was papered with a Hoyle design, while the Bawdens and Hoyle used Marianne Straub's textiles. Because of the extensive reportage of the Bardfield exhibitions, many of these interiors have been recorded. Some of the decorative schemes caused comment even during a period which favoured aggressive colours and bold patterns. *The Daily Telegraph*[6] described Clifford-Smith's hallway as 'fiercely colourful' with the ceiling in shelf paper-like pink checks, grey and white striped walls, blue doors and a grey staircase with blue balusters and a yellow stair carpet. Michael Rothenstein's sitting room, papered with a 'patchwork' of over-printed book jackets and Marianne Straub's cottage beams painted 'out' in white against white walls also received notice (Fig 5.41).

The press coverage of the exhibitions is particularly useful in that it provides a rare assessment of Marianne Straub's work of this period, when too often her industrial production was sold to or seen by a general public unaware of the designer who created it. Of her work *The Times* reported:

'The usual defect of textiles devised by English artists is either that they are too purposefully homespun, or else too self-consciously pretty. These errors Miss Straub has entirely avoided. Her designs are astonishingly rich and, in the very best sense, commercially valid.'[7]

In the introduction to the 1958 exhibition catalogue, Colin MacInnes recorded his impression that 'Her choice of colour is impeccable, her sense of form so harmonious and inventive, that

3 *House and Garden,* July 1955, p60.
4 See Bliss, Douglas Percy *Edward Bawden* Pendomer Press, 1979.
5 MacInnes, Colin *Bardfield Artists* catalogue, 1958, p5.
6 *The Daily Telegraph,* 10 July 1955.
7 *The Times,* 7 July 1955.

her fabrics are radiant of pleasure and delight.' In more anecdotal style, another reporter recalled overhearing 'It's pretty but not pretty pretty'. The reply to this praise was, 'But what would father say? He'd spend 20 years gettng used to it.'[8] Had they but known, 'Father' did have 20 years to get used to it, for many of Marianne Straub's designs of the 1950s remained in pro-

duction for well over a decade. Similarly, interiors decorated in these years, such as the Royal Society of Arts (hung with 'Silverton' in 1953), remained untouched for 20 years.

In 1971, shortly after she retired from Warners, she left her Great Bardfield home to move to Cambridge. Here she was to find time for her own weaving which the combination of

Fig 5.41 Marianne Straub's sitting room in Great Bardfield, 1956. Clockwise from top left are an H.C.Hiscock light, Marianne Straub's 'Broadfield', a Fred Misen corn dolly, Race DA6 settee with cover and cushion by Marianne Straub, Race Antelope chair (in garden), Walter Hoyle wallpaper (by Coles) and painting, Race DA1/IL tub armchair with cover and cushion by Marianne Straub and HK Drake chair with plywood back. The light rug was designed by Gerd Bergerson and the darker rya rug by Marianne Straub for Wallis Mills, Pembrokeshire.

teaching and designing for industry had not allowed. As a result, while in Great Bardfield she had to contend with the gentle chiding of her artist neighbours, who saw one-off pieces as the true mark of originality and would threaten (as only friends can) to categorise her as a 'mere craftsman'. In the ensuing debates she would enthusiastically defend the role of the industrial designer.

The teasing of her neighbours highlights a real difficulty, for any attempt to assess her 20 years at Warners in stylistic terms would be misleading. This is to suggest neither that the appearance of her cloths vacillated wildly nor remained unchanged, but rather that she never wished to create a 'Marianne Straub' style. Brought up to weaving in an era when the cult of the personality was not yet fully formed, she eschewed the title of 'craftsman' and its present association with the individual maker and individual product. Rather, her aim was always to employ the fibres, dyes and looms to produce cloths uniquely suited to their purpose and the style of the end-user or middleman for whom they were made. Her intimate knowledge of her craft resulted in mass-produced textiles with all the hallmarks of handmade cloth: subtlety, texture, warmth and imagination. At Warners she honed these skills to a fine pitch, controlling fibres and techniques to produce cloths with little or more often no figurative element, no *applied* design. In their disciplined and unassuming beauty they are akin to objects of Eastern design which, '. . . while the West lays great stress on the outward form' try to 'depict the spirit of the thing' and are 'therefore less individualistic, less self asserting.'[9] While it is the American textile designer, Dorothy Liebes, who must be credited with innovation in the use of colours in weaves in the post-war period, it is Marianne Straub who did much in that time to establish definitive weaves of quality and content in the language of architects and furniture makers.

8   Hutchins, Patricia 'Artists at Home' *Truth*, 22 July 1955.
9   Harado, Jiro 'A Glimpse of Japanese Ideals' lecture delivered at the University of Washington, 1937, p23.

Beyond industry
Teaching

'For years I said I couldn't teach and then it turns out that if I am ever remembered it's for teaching.'[1]

Marianne Straub began teaching at the age of 47 and always refers to it as her second career. When she took up her first part-time position at the Central School of Art in January 1956, it was with some trepidation. She was persuaded to do so by Mary Kirby and further convinced by the presence of Dora Batty as Head of the textile department at the Central and '. . . an excellent teacher who had all her priorities right'[2] (Fig 6.1). Marianne Straub had refused several offers to teach before:

Fig 6.1 'Batty Bird' printed by Helios c1946 and designed by Dora Batty during her term as Head of the Central School's textile department.

PHOTO JOHN GAY

'Then suddenly one night I thought that it might be a good thing if I handed on some of the experience I had gained in industry. Strangely enough, within a few days of this I had a phone call from the Central School of Arts & Crafts asking me to step into Mary Kirby's place as she was going to teach in Ghana, at Achimoto College. Her departure was at fairly short notice. I accepted the job and then had three weeks of sleepless nights being so anxious about the prospect of teaching. The beginning was indeed difficult because I had to learn so much myself at first, mainly going back to simple things which I had learned to take for granted and had forgotten. But soon I was very happy teaching.'[3]

She brought to her teaching a combination of her wide experience of industrial design, her appreciation of the teaching methods of Heinz Otto Hürlimann and the staff at Bradford Technical College, and her exposure to Ethel Mariet's teaching and philosophy, together with an awareness of continental teaching methods gained on their 1938 European trip. Further, she had served as an examiner on the National Diploma in Design (Fashion/Textiles) committee under the chairmanship of Brian O'Roke Dickey from 1947 to 1959. She already had considerable experience as 'tutor': to Gospels apprentices such as Joyce Griffiths; to Kathleen Fleetwood, who started work at Helios as a design apprentice straight from grammar school; to Joanna Bawden at Warners; and briefly, to John Kitching, who spent three days as Marianne Straub's guest at Great Bardfield while serving a small part of his 'apprenticeship' with her at Warners. Some dozen years later, in 1974, he took his father's place as Managing Director of Parker Knoll Textiles. All three women later took up teaching positions. Joyce Griffiths taught part-time and designed for industry for 25 years while assisting her husband, Hugh Griffiths, who set up a business selling hand-weaving yarns; and she remembers most Marianne Straub's '. . . un-assuming dedication to all aspects of textile production',[4] Kathleen Fleetwood went on to take charge of the wovens section at Bolton College of Art for 27 years and Joanna Bawden taught at the Central, Winchester, Birmingham and Middlesex Polytechnic until she opened her own yarn and dye shop in London.

Marianne Straub quickly became known as an exacting teacher, insisting that her students gain a sound technical knowledge on which to base their creative work. Even before she began teaching she was aware of the problems which faced students and young craftsmen, which she outlined at the 1952 Dartington Hall Conference as:

'. . . the enormous wealth of things available to them. Well, there are all the natural raw materials — all the wools which are a study in themselves, the cotton, the flax, the silk, and on top of all that there are all the artificial yarns which come chasing each other into existence and chasing each other out of existence. All this has to be coped with and there is a tremendous danger there of losing perspective. I would say to all those who teach — concentrate first on one yarn and then on another, not all together. Also, begin by seeing what is the real quality of dead yarn. Let them do plain weave. Let them get the beauty of the plain cloths first and use each yarn separately, and then use them in conjunction.'[5]

She is remembered as always being extremely particular about how the warp was put onto the loom. Her method was to shake and pull the warp as it was wound onto the loom, the most efficient way to free any tangled yarns and now

widely taught. She insisted, too, that the looms be in perfect working order and '. . . would spend ages fixing your loom if something wasn't quite right even if it meant climbing on top or under it!'[6] Her very disciplined attitude to teaching weaving extended to her belief that students must early develop a keen ability to visualise, rather than relying solely on sketches: '. . . they have to get their own television boxes into commission and really see it.'[7]

Her lectures covered woven textile design and technology including Jacquard design and draft-ing, cloth construction and cloth analysis, the latter 'agony at the time' for at least one student, 'but invaluable ever since'.[8] She stressed the importance of becoming a good colourist, because

'. . . when you work for industry . . . you always have to do colour ranges. It's the one thing that students disliked the most and it's only when you start doing it that you realise what a great art it is — it's one of the most time-consuming aspects of industrial design.'[9]

She expected attention to every detail: 'don't forget the selvages!' — a phrase still recalled by a weaver she first taught at Hornsey in 1966.[10] 'Awareness' could well be the key word to summarise what Marianne Straub taught, and since '. . . there is no better way to narrow

1   Interview of Marianne Straub by Margot Coatts, *op cit* p2.
2   Coleman, *op cit* p41.
3   *Ibid.*
4   Correspondence from Joyce Griffiths, *op cit.*
5   Cox (ed), *op cit* p35.
6   Correspondence from Hilary Auden, 16 October 1983.
7   Interview of Marianne Straub by Margot Coatts, *op cit* p9.
8   Correspondence from Wendy Jones, 26 October 1983.
9   Marianne Straub.
10 Correspondence from Wendy Jones, *op cit.*

students' eyes to reality than by instruction from sympathetic but successfully practising artists and designers, and by association with them',[11] to that one should add: the application of common sense.

Marianne Straub remained Head of woven textiles at the Central until 1964, when she began

KETTLE'S YARD

Fig 6.2 'Apron' (1975) by Janet Anderson who was a student of Marianne Straub's at Hornsey in the mid 1960s. She developed a style very different from that of her instructor, as did many of Marianne Straub's students.

teaching at Hornsey (Fig 6.2). In both colleges she taught three days a week, and was always to stress to her students the importance of maintaining the balance between teaching and one's own work. While at Hornsey she hired Mike Halsey as her weave technician. At his interview he was struck with her acute memory for people, their work and their interests, for she remembered not only him, but his work at college which she had assessed some years previously.[12] He remained at Hornsey for three years and developed a great regard for her vast store of knowledge. In 1968 she left Hornsey for the Royal College of Art, teaching one day a week for the first year then, until her retirement in 1974, two days. Three of the six weave students in her first year at the RCA she had also taught at Hornsey (Rita James, Wendy Jones and Fay Morgan). From

Fig. 6.3 Detail of an all-cotton drawloom woven sample by Amelia Uden, c1979. She began to develop this form of brocading while a student of Marianne Straub's at the RCA in 1969–71.

these students Amelia Uden, one among the remaining three, gained '. . . an impression of this person, whom I had, as yet, never met — an impression of a very strong character who had instilled in all her students a sense of purpose, a considerable knowledge of cloth construction and above all an ability to work hard.' (Fig 6.3)[13]

Marianne Straub encouraged her students by working hard herself: '. . . she was always available when help was needed, nothing was too much trouble for her and no job was too small or tedious.' (Fig 6.4)[14] And she earned the respect of her students through her treatment of each as an individual, giving information and direction

when needed, as each student was able to absorb it. When asked she would give detailed advice. Criticism, when offered, was always constructive, and she always acknowledged the students' own opinions. Stopford Jacks, external examiner of Marianne Straub's students at the Central and

11 Darwin, Robin, 'The Double Dividend' *Design* 134, February 1950, p50, a report of an exhibition by LCC Central School of Arts & Crafts design staff, autumn 1949, in which Marianne Straub participated.
12 Telephone interview with Mike Malsey, 7 Nov 1983.
13 Correspondence from Amelia Uden, 4 October 1983.
14 Correspondence from Mary Restieaux, 26 Oct 1983.
15 Correspondence from Stopford Jacks, *op cit.*

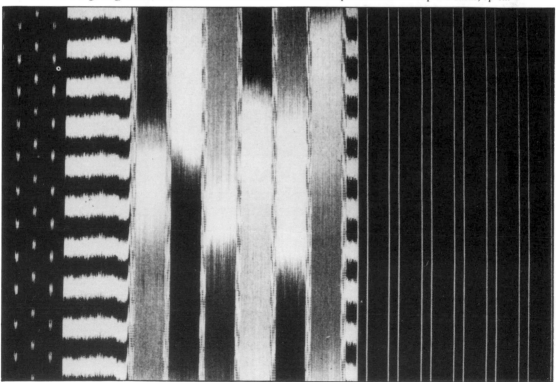

Fig 6.4 An ikat and space-dyed all-spun silk cloth, c1979, by Mary Restieaux, one of Marianne Straub's students at the RCA in 1972–74.

Hornsey, saw that, '... she never imposed herself upon them, they were encouraged to express themselves — but the basis of their training was very sound.'[15] Others observed that 'she really did inspire everyone in the weave departments at Central and Hornsey.'[16] Her later years as a teacher witnessed a trend away from greater numbers of students as passionately interested in the craft of weaving (Fig 6.5). During the 1970s students at the RCA who increasingly used their knowledge of weaving as a styling tool found their interest in high-fashion 'ephemera' fabrics out of sympathy with Marianne Straub's classic,

well constructed cloths. To many, however, Marianne Straub imparted her own approach to designing. Wendy Jones (Lecturer and Weaver of Rugs and Furnishing Fabrics) explains:

'Under her guidance I was taught how to teach myself, how to explore and understand the structure of woven fabrics... [I learned] a thorough understanding of designing the whole fabric, starting with visual ideas through to creating the woven structures.'[17]

Mike Halsey became a teacher with the encour-

Fig 6.5 A doublecloth rug displayed by Rita James at the RCA's student exhibition, 1970. The traditional format is wittily interpreted through the use of a warp of mercerised cotton and a weft of one-inch wide India tape dyed by the designer.

agement of Marianne Straub, who made him more conscious of technique and the importance of asking 'why?' and not just 'how?', so that known techniques could be exploited in new ways.

Marianne Straub was, herself, involved in new technology, working jointly on computer-aided textile design with Professor Malcolm Burnip, then a lecturer at Manchester University Institute of Science and Technology. When he later visited the Royal College to lecture on non-woven fabrics; the 'connections' for the design students between his explanations of the technology and the designer's viewpoint were made by Marianne Straub. When Burnip moved to Huddersfield on the formation of the Polytechnic, he and Roger Nicholson, Head of the textile department of the RCA

'. . . agreed to stage a yarn design course at Huddersfield sponsored by the Worshipful Company of Weavers. Marianne came with the students from the Royal College to assist my staff. The association with Huddersfield grew from there and with it a warm personal relationship.'[18]

This friendship was to have a subsequent impact on the course at Huddersfield (see page 000).

She also took a personal interest in her students which extended beyond their college days. Two students, Jeremy Talbot (designer for his own firm and previously Director of Edward Pond Associates) and Andrea Mossiman-Grass (freelance printed textile designer) worked for Warners in Braintree during or after the completion of their courses at the Central (Fig 6.6). Marianne Straub has followed the careers of all her ex-students with great interest, giving encouragement and when asked, advice. Of those who went on to teach part-time (there are a score or more), most carried her philosophy to the next generation of students. Hilary Auden, weaver of

'cloth for a purpose' and Lecturer at the Central says:

'Because weaving can be extremely time consuming and incomprehensible when you

COURTESY OF WARNER & SONS LTD

Fig 6.6 'Fern & Leaf, designed by Andrea Mossiman-Grass at Warners in 1956.

16 Telephone conversation with Eileen Ellis, 10 June 1984.
17 Correspondence from Wendy Jones, *op cit.*
18 Correspondence from Prof Malcolm Burnip, 4 November 1983.

first start, and students can easily be put off, I go out of my way to encourage and help with the numerous technical difficulties that can occur before you even start weaving! I always try to think of how Marianne Straub encouraged me at various ups and downs of my career (the teaching didn't stop when I left college) and try to do the same for my students.'[19]

Fig 6.7 Marianne Straub in a Kay Cosserat knitted jacket given to her by the designer. Designed in 1982, it employs a wide variety of natural-fibre yarns with edgings and appliqued strips of frayed tweed.

To those who went into industry she passed on her experience and her example as a successful designer, summed up by Misha Black in 1954 as someone who, '. . . must be an expert technician, a good organiser, have the personality which will ensure him a proper hearing at managerial level, and the relentless tenacity which will enable him to fight for what he considers the proper design solution.'[20]

Her students were equally successful in areas less directly associated with Marianne Straub's own dual arena of industrial design and teaching, becoming print designers, knitters, and makers of one-off wovens. Designers in the latter two categories cite Marianne Straub's intense interest in fibres and cloth handle as lasting influences. The knitter, Kay Cosserat, remarking that an appreciation of the quality and handle of fabrics always plays an extremely important part when designing knitted fabrics (Fig 6.7), added that she '. . . first became aware of fabric quality under Marianne's guidance.'[21]

If an industrial designer's measure of success is sales, the measure of a teacher must be in the friendships and loyalties which remain long after students have themselves become professionals. In Marianne Straub's case, the friendships are many and the praise they give her is enthusiastic. They cite her professionalism, dedication, generosity, and open-mindedness; her sensitive and sensible attitude towards her work and her students; and her ability to accept a situation and use it to its best advantage. She produced no 'disciples of style' but rather independent, creative designers, many of whom have since contributed significantly to their own field.

19   Correspondence from Hilary Auden, *op cit.*
20   Black, Misha, 'The Value of Good Design', from *A Report on the Scottish Design Congress*, Alistair Maynard (ed), Edinburgh 1954, p34.
21   Correspondence from Kay Cosserat, 24 October 1983.

Consultancy

Since her retirement from the Royal College in 1974 Marianne Straub has continued to teach as a visiting lecturer at the Royal College, the Central, Goldsmith's College, Brighton Polytechnic, Huddersfield Polytechnic, Liverpool College of Art, West Surrey College of Art and Design and elsewhere (Fig 6.8). In addition she has lectured to weavers' guilds, Quarry Bank Mill (Styal, Cheshire), the Craft Study Centre in Bath, Highland Craftpoint and at numerous workshops throughout the United Kingdom. In 1979 she undertook a lecture tour of Australia and New Zealand.

Through her work on the Coldstream textile design panel and as a specialist advisor to its successor in 1973, the CNAA (Council for National Academic Awards), she has helped to raise the standard of textile design education during a period when the structure of Diploma and BA courses has been radically altered. From the mid 1960s she has served as an external examiner for nine colleges' weaving courses,[1] the most recent of which is Camberwell College of Art. She has also been actively involved in the development of the combined textile design and technology BSc course at Huddersfield Polytechnic, introduced in the autumn of 1977. The course has been developed by a team headed by Professor Malcolm Burnip, Head of the Department of Textile Technology:

> 'Searching for the means of developing the department and conscious, perhaps because of coming from a university, of the "equal to but different from" syndrome of polytechnics, the idea of a textile design course which attempted to integrate and infuse textile design with technology was slowly formulating. For a designer to have such ideas might then have seemed peculiar, but for a textile engineer to have them was obviously heretical! I was sustained in all of this by Marianne, who became the Polytechnic's consultant and with whom I could discuss all my faltering or outrageous ideas which eventually became the BSc (Hons)

PHOTO CHRIS HUNT

Fig 6.8 Details of a silk and cotton brocaded panel by Anne Crowley, who studied weaving at the RCA from 1975 to 1977. Marianne Straub was a visiting lecturer during these years and aided the designer in developing the use of brocading on a multiple shaft woven ground.

1   These colleges and polytechnics are Liverpool, Manchester and Birmingham (three years on each of two occasions); Belfast, Farnham and the Royal College (three years each); Derby, Lonsdale and Winchester (one year each) and Camberwell (a three year commitment commencing in '82/83). She never assessed at more than two colleges in the same year.

Textile Design sandwich degree at Huddersfield Polytechnic. If the staff expected I could sustain them through setbacks and disappointments of the course's early development, including the massive shock of the deaths within the first 18 months of two course tutors, it was Marianne who by telephone, by letter laboriously written, or by working visits sustained me.'[2]

Her support of the course came from her conviction that it would give a rigorous, balanced training, and she applied herself to her role as consultant with characteristic energy, taking up, in addition, the task of advisor to students supervised by Professor Burnip in CNAA research degree work. Professor Burnip continues:

'A working visit to her meant working with the students from early morning to early evening, seeing each one individually, talking to staff and then talking to me until late at night about her feelings on developments. Always positive, always pointing to new possibilities, she was a sound critic whose advice was always clear and helpful.'[3]

For her hours of labour the only reward she anticipates is 'its successes' which '. . . will give me great satisfaction.'[4]

In 1971 Marianne Straub had moved to Cambridge and set up a studio in her home, where she produced a number of commissioned works. She continued to design for Tamesa until 1975, although less frequently than she had while at Warners, and designed a second London Transport Underground upholstery cloth for the DRU in 1973. 'One-off' projects became a possibility when she ceased working for industry and the first such commission came from the architects, Robert, Matthew, Johnson, and Marshall for the Gwent Police Headquarters building, completed in 1971. For the entry hall of

the building she produced a group of five wool banners, each 180 by 42 inches. Their impact is derived from bold, graphic shapes employing contrasts in colour and texture. A second set of four banners, designed on similar principles, was commissioned by Wilson and Wornersley for the Huddersfield Polytechnic Central Services building, opened in 1977 (see colour section). The design was dyed and warped on the numerically programmable warper in the textile department. Woven in New Zealand crossbred wools it comprises, 'almost as a lesson in woven fabric structures'[5] a number of complex and compound weaves.

Fig 6.9 The Roman auxiliary soldier at the Housesteads Site Museum, wearing a cloak reproduced by Marianne Straub in 1981.

In 1981 she undertook the study of extant examples of Roman weaving in order to accurately reproduce a cloak for a model of a Roman auxiliary soldier at the Housesteads Site Museum, administered by the Department of Archaeology of the University of Newcastle (Fig 6.9). She analysed fibre, spin, dye and cloth construction in consultation with Dr John Peter Wild of Manchester University and Miss L. Allason-Jones of the University of Newcastle. The resulting seven feet square cloak, hand-woven of handspun natural 'mooret' brown North Ronaldsey fleece is '. . . magnificent and possibly the closest reproduction of Roman weaving in Britain.'[6] Shortly afterwards she completed a similar project for the Colebridge Museum, also under the aegis of the University of Newcastle. Employing handspun Ryland fleece hank dyed with madder, she produced a red tunic for a Roman Centurion and in addition a hand-woven undyed linen neckerchief. Her interest in Roman-British weaving led to an invitation to join the 'Early Textiles Study Group' as an honorary member.

Marianne Straub continues to weave in her studio, although she finds that the freedom of non-industrial design is often more of an obstacle than an asset. Most recently she has woven a handful of lengths for inclusion in a retrospective exhibition of her work organised and sponsored by Warner & Sons Ltd and travelling throughout the UK in 1984 and '85.

Because she was so long an industrial designer her work has been represented in numerous trade shows, 'theme' exhibitions and group exhibitions in that context.[7] It was not until 1981, when David Pye selected one of her pieces for inclusion in 'The Maker's Eye' at the Crafts Council Gallery (Jan-May 1982), that her work was assessed from the craftsman's point of view. David Pye's choice of pieces (he was one of 14 selectors) was based on his view that:

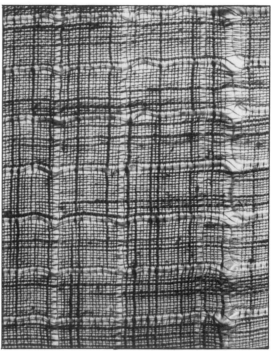

Fig 6.10 A detail of an untitled hanging by Marianne Straub, 1980, hand-woven in pure silk employing the linked warp technique. This piece was included by David Pye in his selection of works for the Craft Council's 'Maker's Eye' exhibition in 1981.

2   Correspondence from Prof Malcolm Burnip, *op cit.*
3   *Ibid.*
4   Coleman, *op cit* p42.
5   Correspondence from Prof Malcolm Burnip, *op cit.*
6   Correspondence from L. Allason-Jones, 3 October 1983.
7   Theme exhibitions include 'The Thirties' (Hayward Gallery 1979) and 'Homespun to Highspeed' (Sheffield City Art Galleries 1979); group exhibitions include the Great Bardfield and Colour, Design & Style Centre exhibitions (already mentioned), 'Choice of Design' (a Warners travelling exhibition 1981/2), 'Design since 1945' (Philadelphia Museum of Modern Art 1983) and 'Texstyles' (Crafts Council 1984).

'The fine arts, the crafts and industrial production are manifestly all parts of one continuum ... Paul Valery wrote of architecture that there are some buildings which speak and some which are dumb; but there are some which sing. In selecting things for this exhibition, I have selected things which sing ... things which are not only of good design but of good workmanship also. A finely designed thing made with bad workmanship is like good music badly played — intolerable.'[8]

The piece was handwoven in pure undyed silk and employed a linked warp technique, invented by Marianne Straub. This is a process by which separately weighted warp threads (ends) are caught by a weft thread (pick) and drawn sideways into the cloth. The deflection of warp threads can occur at any point in the weaving and may therefore be used to create a random or repeat pattern on both plain or simply textured cloths (Fig 6.10). It was in 1981 also that Kettle's Yard originated a travelling exhibition, 'Textiles Today', selected and introduced by Marianne

KETTLE'S YARD

Figs 6.11 and 6.11a Two of the pieces selected by Marianne Straub for 'Textiles Today', demonstrating 'the wide range of things made by the interweaving of threads on either a loom or some sort of frame'. (Left) Sarah Bungey's bonded, cut out and fringed experiment, c1979, and (right) Archie Brennan's high-warp tapestry 'For the Summer of '75', c1975.

Straub. The catalogue essay gives evidence of her own catholic tastes:

'Cloths which have a functional purpose, rugs, quilts and so forth, interest me as much as textiles which are conceived to hang on the wall'

and the difficulties attendant upon discussion of these:

'Sadly, our vocabulary lacks a word which will meaningfully embrace the wide range of things made by the interweaving of threads on either a loom or some sort of frame.' (Figs 6.11 & 6.11a)

It provides, too, her views on the demarcation between artists and craftsmen, giving at the same time the philosophical essence of her own work:

'Every artist embodies in his work the craftsmanship of execution, and every creative craftsman is involved with questions of aesthetic judgement and originality in taking his work beyond the boundaries of pure function and skill.'[9]

Such published personal comments are rare; her full-length work is a practical handbook, *Handweaving and Cloth Design*,[10] named 'Best Crafts Book of the Year' by the Crafts Council in 1977. Writing it was an arduous task for one whose form of communication is lively discussion, but she undertook it because her main interest now '. . . is to hand on whatever knowledge I have gained.'[11] In her introductory note she reiterates what, as a teacher, she espoused, saying:

'I believe that by thoroughly comprehending the methods by which weave constructions are evolved, the traditional theories of cloth design can constantly be reassessed in the light of a more adventurous attitude to fabrics and the availability of a changing range of yarns.'[12]

Fig 6.12 Marianne Straub's living room, Cambridge 1984. In the right foreground is a Race prototype chair, a gift of Ernest Race, later re-covered with 'Samson' a Marianne Straub/ Warners/Tamesa fabric. Most of the non-European textiles, including the Turkish cloths covering the Race sofa and Parker Knoll chair, were collected during her travels since 1970. Also of note: (from left) the painting by Walter Hoyle, the Fishley jug, the curtains ('Coppelia' by Marianne Straub), the hand-woven hand-spun linen tablecloth by Percy Beale and the Henry Hammond bowl.

8   Pye, D. *The Maker's Eye*, Crafts Council, London, 1981.
9   *Textiles Today*, Kettle's Yard, Cambridge, 1981. Introduction by Marianne Straub December 1980, p8.
10 Straub, Marianne *Handweaving and Cloth Design* Pelham Press, 1977. The link warp technique was invented for this publication and is outlined on pp89-90.
11 Coleman, *op cit* p42.
12 Straub, *op cit* p8.

Her reference to 'traditional theories of cloth design' embraces her growing first-hand knowledge of the weaving practices of non-Europeans, for travel is another interest which she had been able to develop since she retired from Warners. While designing for industry she was unable to make extended trips, which excluded travel beyond Europe. Moreover, '. . . when I was young I was most interested in developing my own ideas — I felt I had to get them out of my system. Now I enjoy travelling greatly and seeing things from many parts of the world, and getting to know how they were made.' (Fig 6.12)[13]

In 1973 she made the first of four trips to Mexico to stay with an ex-Central student (1959–62) Valerie Searle, who was a 'brilliant teacher'[14] at the London College of Furniture before moving to a small village in Yucatan close to the Belise border, to make hammocks. Two years later a Sanderson's travel grant financed a visit to Guatemala, where she studied Indian cloths and learned to use a back-strap loom. For the World Bank, she spent two weeks in Mali in 1979, investigating ways in which the local weaving crafts tradition could be supported. She suggested that they revive a small rug weaving establishment in Segou, on the Niger, and as a result, a co-operative was formed with the assistance of Christian Aid (Fig 9.6). Her other travels have taken her to Thailand, the USSR and China; and everywhere she has been saddened by the way in which traditional crafts are being undermined:

'It is heartbreaking that as soon as tourists appear on the scene, and the local people start to weave for sale, and not only for their own needs, the standard of workmanship, colour and design deteriorate . . . We are losing so much by the way of standards and know-how of techniques.'[15]

It is Marianne Straub's deep concern for standards of excellence in design and support of all those, who like her, work to maintain them, that have characterised her 50 years as designer and teacher. Long regarded as one of the avant garde by her peers and widely respected by leaders in her own field (Alastair Morton '. . . always said that Marianne was the best handweaver/designer in the country'[16]), late in her life these qualities were acknowledged by her receipt of the title 'Royal Designer for Industry' (RDI) from the Royal Society of Arts in 1972 (Fig 6.14), the first design medal awarded by the Textile Institute in 1972, and the Jubilee Medal in 1977. By her friends, colleagues and students, however, she is not only respected for her great love of weaving, but also for her seemingly endless energy and enthusiasm for all that she

Fig 6.13 A Mali blanket of the type which was used by Marianne Straub to inspire a revival of traditional designs at the rug-weaving workshop in Segou.

13 Coleman, *op cit* p42.
14 Marianne Straub.
15 Coleman, *op cit* p42.
16 Correspondence from Cherry (Mrs Alastair) Morton, 6 May 1984. I am also indebted to Jacqueline Groag, who confirmed these points.

Fig 6.14 Marianne Straub photographed by DESIGN magazine on receipt of her RDI in 1972.

undertakes, and her generosity, both with her knowledge and her time. Joyce Griffiths relates that when her husband began selling yarns for handweavers and embroiderers he was given the names of several suppliers by Ethel Mairet and that:

> 'Marianne gave him the addresses of two Welsh Mills with whom we traded for over 30 years and later on she gave us help over cottons and firms of dyers. In fact she 'made' the Hugh Griffith business and always helped us however busy she was.'[17]

For others, her generosity extended further. Kathleen Fleetwood speaks for many when she acknowledges,

> '. . . a great debt of gratitude to Miss Straub — not only for the knowledge, skills and attitudes of mind which I learned at Helios — but also, during the early years of my employment, for the introduction to other areas of cultural and creative activity and interest, which broadened my horizons and enriched my later life.'[18]

At 74, Marianne Straub remains active: 'Godmother' to her 'last, *great* interest',[19] the Huddersfield BSc course, for which '. . . the advice, the new ideas and the criticism — always constructive and always well considered — continues with enthusiasm';[20] she remains an external examiner, a Trustee of the Crafts Study Centre in Bath; and is still weaving, still lecturing, still travelling. That she continues to do so is a tribute to her character — determined but unassuming — and her ready humour and empathy. She shies from accepting praise and is quick to name other designers and teachers who also contributed much to the field of textiles and design. Nevertheles, she is regarded by many as the finest weaver of her era and, by those who know her, as one who greatly improves the quality of life of the people she meets.

---

17 Correspondence from Joyce Griffiths, *op cit.*
18 Correspondence from Kathleen Fleetwood, *op cit.*
19 Marianne Straub.
20 Correspondence from Prof Malcolm Burnip, *op cit.*

Further reading

The books listed below are those of prime importance to the main topics covered. Most contain extensive bibliographies and/or information on the location of primary source material.

Allwood A. & Laurie K. *R.D. Russell, Marian Peplar,* Catalogue, ILEA, 1983.

Arts Council of Great Britain. *Thirties: British Art and Design before the War,* Catalogue, London, 1980.

Baynes K. & K. *Gordon Russell,* Design Council, London, 1981.

Bury, H. *Alec B. Hunter,* Catalogue, Warner & Sons Ltd, London, 1979.

Bury, H. *A Choice of Design,* Catalogue, Warner & Sons Ltd, London 1981.

Camden Arts Centre. *Enid Marx,* Catalogue, London, 1979.

Carrington, N. *Industrial Design in Britain,* Allen & Unwin, London, 1976.

Coatts, M. *A Weaver's Life: Ethel Mairet 1872–1952,* Crafts Council, London, 1983.

Conway, H. *Ernest Race,* Design Council, London, 1982.

Coulson, A.J. *A Bibliography of Design in Britain: 1851–1970,* Design Council, London, 1979.

Council of Industrial Design. *Design 46: Survey of British Industrial Design as Displayed at the 'Britain Can Make It' Exhibition,* HMSO, London, 1946.

Cox, P. (ed) *Dartington Hall International Conference on Pottery and Textiles 1952,* Transcript, Dartington, 1954.

Crafts Council. *The Maker's Eye,* Catalogue, London, 1981.

Crankshaw, W.P. *Report on a survey of the Welsh woollen industry made on behalf of the University of Wales,* University of Wales, 1927.

Farr, M. *Design in British Industry: a Mid-Century Survey,* Cambridge University Press, 1953.

Festival of Britain, Catalogue of Exhibits, HMSO, London, 1951.

Goodale, E. *Weaving and the Warners,* F. Lewis Publishers Ltd, London, 1971.

Jenkins, J.C. *The Welsh Woollen Industry,* National Museum of Wales, Welsh Folk Museum, Cardiff, 1969.

Kettle's Yard. *Textiles Today,* Catalogue, Cambridge, 1981.

MacCarthy, F. *British Design Since 1880,* Lund Humphries, London, 1982.

MacCarthy, F. *A History of British Design 1830–1979,* Allen & Unwin, London, 1979.

Mairet, E. *Handweaving Today: Traditions & Changes,* Faber & Faber, London, 1939.

Martin, J.L. & Speight, S. *The Flat Book,* William Heinemann Ltd, London, 1939.

Morton, J. *Three Generations in a Family Textile Firm,* Routledge & Kegan Paul, London, 1971.

Pevsner, N. *An enquiry into industrial art in England,* Cambridge University Press, 1937.

Read, H. *Art & Industry: the principles of industrial design,* Faber & Faber, London, 1934.

Scottish National Gallery of Modern Art. *Alastair Morton and Edinburgh Weavers: Abstract Art and Textile Design 1933–46,* Catalogue, Edinburgh, 1978.

Society of Industrial Artists. *Designers in Britain,* Vols 1–6, SIA/Alan Wingate, London, 1947–64.

Straub, M. *Handweaving and Cloth Design,* Pelham Press, London, 1977.

Wood, H.T. *History of the Royal Society of Arts,* Murray, 1913.

Woodham, J.M. *Industrial Design and the Public,* Pembridge Press, London.

MAGAZINES

Ambassador
Architectural Review
Art and Industry
Cabinet Maker
Crafts
Decoration
Design
Design for Today
Fashion and Fabric Overseas
Furnishing Fabrics
Progressive Architecture
The Studio
Journal of the Royal Society of Arts
Journal of the Rural Industries Bureau
Journal of the Royal Institute of British Architects
Textiles International

Acknowledgements

I did not know Marianne Straub when I began writing her biography, and the greatest pleasure in doing so has been coming to know her well. The depth and breadth of her knowledge — indicated but not contained within these pages— is enormous, surpassed only by her enthusiasm and patience in the face of my unrelenting questions. I am indeed indebted to her, and hope that the result of our collaboration will be seen as her work as much as mine.

Much of the information in Marianne's story has been gathered from others who took part; to all those who communicated with me in person, by telephone or in writing I owe a great debt of thanks: L. Allason Jones, Hilary Auden, Edward and Joanna Bawden, Lady Black, Hilary Bourne, Sarah Bungey, Malcolm Burnip, Trevor Chinn, N.J. Colgate, Kay Cosserat, Frederick Dickenson, Sir Geoffrey Dunn, Eileen Ellis, Barry and Luccia Ercolani, Kathleen Fleetwood, A.V. Freeman, Beryl Gibson, Sir Ernest Goodale, Andrea Mossiman Grass, Jacqueline Groag, Sir Milner Grey, Eifion Griffith, Joyce Griffiths, Mike Halsey, Peter Hall, Anthony Heal, Stopford Jacks, Wendy Jones, Margery Kendon, Margerie Kenney, Douglas and John Kitching, Sir William Mansfield Cooper, Cherry Morton, Janet Oliver, E.R. Patterson, E.J. Power, Mary Restieaux, Aubrey Ricketts, Sheila Robinson, Lesley Smith, L.J. Smith, Monika Veenhoff-Stadler, Ruth Straub, Jeremy Talbot, Isabell Tisdell, Donald Tomlinson, Amelia Uden, Alan Wheeler, Charles Williams, David Wiltshire and Elizabeth Wray.

I would also like to acknowledge those who aided me in my research towards both this book and the accompanying exhibition: Rosamond Allwood and Kedrun Laurie, Geoffrye Museum; Nick Arber, Crafts Council Gallery; Antonia Austin, Central School of Art; Deborah Barker; Michael Clare, Bradford & Ilkley Community College; Frank Davis and Chris Williams, Warner & Sons Ltd; Janet Elliott, CoSIRA Librarian; Jean Harding, SIAD Librarian; Jennifer Harris and Maude Wallace, Whitworth Art Gallery; Robin Hartley, Heal's; Robert Howell, V&A Archive; Alan James, BBC Architects' Department; Sarah Levitt and Jane Tozer, Gallery of English Costume; Valerie Mendez, V&A Textile Department; Barley Roscoe, Crafts Study Centre and Margot Coatts, whose research notes on Ethel Mairet and transcripts of interviews with Marianne Straub, Hilary Bourne, Joyce Griffiths, Marjory Kendon and Margorie Kenney (held at the Craft Study Centre) were an invaluable source of information. The Design Council staff were extremely helpful throughout and I would particularly like to thank Terry Bishop, Paul Burrell, Sylvia Katz, Bridget Kinally, Tim Quallington, photographer, and the editor of this text, Jony Russell. Finally, it is a great pleasure to have the opportunity to acknowledge the generosity of L. St. J. Tibbitts, Chairman of Warner & Sons Ltd., whose support and guidance has made this project possible and my work as Archivist at Warners so enjoyable.